Income Inequality in Korea

An Analysis of Trends, Causes, and Answers

This volume is part of the multivolume study
Rising to the Challenge of Democratization and Globalization in Korea,
1987–2007

Harvard East Asian Monographs 354

Income Inequality in Korea

An Analysis of Trends, Causes, and Answers

Chong-Bum An

and

Barry Bosworth

Published by the Harvard University Asia Center
and distributed by Harvard University Press
Cambridge (Massachusetts) and London, 2013

Printed in the United States of America

The Harvard University Asia Center publishes a monograph series and, in coordination with the Fairbank Center for Chinese Studies, the Korea Institute, the Reischauer Institute of Japanese Studies, and other faculties and institutes, administers research projects designed to further scholarly understanding of China, Japan, Vietnam, Korea, and other Asian countries. The Center also sponsors projects addressing multidisciplinary and regional issues in Asia.

Library of Congress Cataloging-in-Publication Data

An, Chong-Bum, 1959–
    Income inequality in Korea : an analysis of trends, causes, and answers / [Chong-Bum An, Barry P. Bosworth].
        pages cm. — (Harvard East Asian monographs ; 354)
    "This volume is part of the multivolume study Rising to the Challenge of Democratization and Globalization in Korea, 1987–2007."
    Includes bibliographical references and index.
    Summary: "Explores the relationship between economic growth and social developments in Korea over the last three decades. Analyzes the forces behind the trends in the narrowing of income distribution in the 1980s and early 1990s, and the deterioration evident in the post financial crisis years"—Provided by publisher.
    ISBN 978-0-674-07319-7 (hardcover : alk. paper) 1. Income distribution—Korea (South) 2. Economic development—Korea (South) 3. Korea (South)—Economic conditions. 4. Korea (South)—Social conditions. I. Bosworth, Barry, 1942– II. Title.
    HC470.I5A52 2013

    339.2095195—dc23   2012050271

    Index by Enid Zafran

    ∞ Printed on acid-free paper

Last figure below indicates year of this printing

23   22   21   20   19   18   17   16   15   14   13

Acknowledgments

We would like to thank the Korean Development Institute for its support during the preparation of the manuscript. We also would like to express our appreciation to Gary Fields, Louis Kuijs, Myung Jae Sung, Byung-In Lim, and an anonymous referee, who provided helpful comments on preliminary versions of the study. Aaron Flaaen, Rosanna Smart, Jiun Jung, Seohyun Lee, and Sveta Milusheva provided excellent research assistance. Gretchen O'Connor and Kathleen Burke helped with preparation of the manuscript.

Contents

Tables and Figures

Tables

Figures

Income Inequality in Korea

An Analysis of Trends, Causes, and Answers

CHAPTER 1

Introduction and Summary

In the early 1990s, Korea was often showcased as a country that had combined extraordinary rates of economic growth with a narrowing of the income distribution.[1] As such, it appeared to refute a famous hypothesis of Simon Kuznets suggesting that, beginning from low levels of income per capita, inequality would increase with rising incomes and begin to diminish only in the later stages of economic development. Korea also exhibited strong gains in other dimensions of economic welfare, reducing the rate of unemployment to a remarkably low 2 percent of the work force by the mid-1990s and achieving relatively low rates of poverty. Korea was frequently cited in support of a new hypothesis positing a positive relationship between growth and social equity.[2]

However, in the years following the 1997–1998 financial crisis, the income distribution has deteriorated—returning to the levels of inequality exhibited in the early 1980s—unemployment soared for an extended period, and rates of poverty have risen to levels well above those of the pre-crisis era. Furthermore, within Korea the public's perceptions of the progress toward reducing social and economic inequalities have been consistently less favorable than those of foreign observers, and opinion

---

1. See Birdsall, Ross, and Sabot (1995); Leipziger, Dollar, and Shorrocks (1992).

2. See, for example, Alesina and Rodrik (1994), Persson and Tabellini (1994), and Perotti (1996). Alesina and Rodrik emphasize political and economic factors that would create a positive correlation. An economy's growth rate and the distribution of incomes are endogenous outcomes that are subject to common influences, and it seems unlikely that the relationship between the two is stable without specifying the underlying policies and other conditions that drive them.

polls reflect a belief that the gap between the rich and the poor has widened over time—a belief that has intensified since the 1997–1998 crisis.[3] Economic recovery and aggressive efforts to expand the size of the public welfare system have not brought an end to the increase in inequality.

This volume explores the historical development of the relationship between economic growth and social developments in Korea. Can we account for the shift toward growing income inequality since the crisis, and have government social welfare policies been effective in slowing or offsetting that trend? The most fundamental questions are whether the pre-crisis pattern of combining strong economic growth with improving equality can be restored, and how government policies might be designed to promote that objective. Thus, we need to understand the forces behind both the equalizing trends in the 1980s and early 1990s and the deterioration that is so evident in the post-crisis years. This will entail an examination of the role of macroeconomic conditions, gains in educational attainment, demographic changes and conditions in labor markets, and the role of social welfare policies.

Our analysis is largely confined to the years after the June 1987 uprising and the historic shift to a democratic government in Korea. While the political shift was quite profound, our focus on the post-1987 period is also motivated by the shortage of available survey data on income for earlier decades. A small family-income and expenditure survey was started in the 1950s, but it was limited to urban wage-earner households throughout most of its history and the micro-level data sets are available only for 1982 and later years. Much of the early work on the distribution of income across all households relies on various methods of extrapolating income from wage-earner to non-wage-earner households. In some cases the extension was based on inferences from surveys of consumption. We provide a summary of the existing research on the earlier period in which estimates of income inequality have been extended back to the mid-1960s, but our focus is on the more recent period.

---

3. According to a 2008 British Broadcasting Corporation poll conducted in 34 major countries, the perception that the benefits and burdens of economic development have not been fairly distributed in the respondent's country was highest among South Koreans (86 percent). Poll results (BBC 2008) are available at: http://www.worldpublicopinion .org/pipa/pdf/feb08/BBCEcon_Feb08_rpt.pdf.

In Part I of our study we assess empirical measures of the change in income distribution over the past two decades. This incorporates information on the macroeconomic distribution of income among the household, government, and business sectors and micro-survey data on the size distribution of wages and total incomes within the household sector. We document a major improvement in income equality up to the mid-1990s, and a significant deterioration since the outbreak of the financial crisis and its continuation in the face of the subsequent economic recovery. We also provide information on trends at the bottom of the income distribution by analyzing various measures of poverty.

The second portion of the book focuses on efforts to account for the patterns of change in the distribution of income and poverty, by examining the role of various socioeconomic determinants. These include an examination of Simon Kuznets's hypothesis of a negative relationship between economic growth and income equality in the early stages of development, the influence of business-cycle fluctuations, globalization, demographic change, education, and labor market institutions. An understanding of the causes of the deterioration in the income distribution is critical to the design of policies to reverse it.

The third section examines the effectiveness of the redistributive policies of the public sector and the role of public expenditure and tax programs aimed at influencing the distribution of economic welfare. These include the public pension system, health care, employment security, welfare assistance and the structure of the income tax system. We conclude with a discussion of some proposals for improving the efficacy of redistributive policies in Korea.

A Brief Summary

Until the mid-1990s, the experience of Korea seemed to support the view that reduced levels of income inequality and a strong focus on improvements in social welfare were fully compatible with and even supported rapid economic growth. However, the hypothesis of a strong reinforcing association of growth and equity seems more questionable in the aftermath of the financial crisis, when economic recovery was not matched by a reversal of the trend toward greater inequality. Has there been a structural break in that relationship, and, if so, what factors are responsible for the deterioration? How has the government responded to the changed circumstances, and have the policy actions been effective? Fear of rising inequality is a major concern of those who argue against increased integration with the global economy, and it motivates calls for an enlarged public welfare system. In the remainder of this chapter, we summarize some of our major findings with regard to these key issues.

MEASURING INEQUALITY AND POVERTY

Our analysis of trends in the distribution of income is focused on the post-1987 period, when Korea experienced a vigorous democratic movement and growing concerns about social welfare. Figure 1.1 displays the trend in the income distribution as measured by the Gini coefficient for urban worker households. While it excludes a large proportion of the population, it appears to be representative of the broader measures and serves to highlight the basic pattern of a gradual improvement up until the mid-1990s, followed by a very large deterioration in the years of financial crisis that is not reversed with economic recovery. In Chapter 2 we examine alternative measures of income equality and expand the analysis to include more encompassing measures of households. However, the basic pattern remains—particularly the sustained increase in income inequality after 1997.

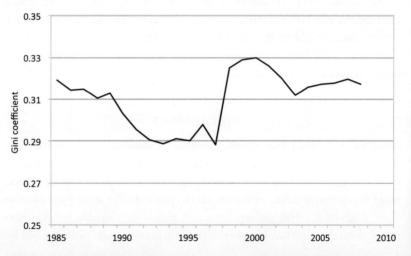

Figure 1.1. The Gini Coefficient for Income Inequality in Korea, 1985–2008
Source: Authors' estimates are based on the micro-data files of the Household Income and Expenditure Survey (Korea National Statistical Office 2009).

At the level of the macro-economy, the primary problem is that the return to high rates of economic growth after the crisis, as measured by the changes in gross domestic product (GDP), has not been matched by comparable growth in household incomes. A major reason for the reduced gains has been a fall in the household share of aggregate income. The share of GDP accounted for by corporate profits has expanded well beyond its pre-crisis level, and together with large government budget surpluses, this has limited the flow of income to households. The household share of gross national income declined from 68 percent in the years 1988–1997 to an average of only 60 percent in 2001–2006. In addition, households have been experiencing major losses of purchasing power as the prices of the consumer products they purchase have been rising more rapidly than the prices of the goods and services they produce—a loss in their terms of trade. As a result of both of these factors, per capita real disposable income over the period from 2000 to 2006 grew at only one-third the rate of GDP per capita—1.3 percent versus 4.2 percent per year.

In addition, the narrowing of the distribution of incomes within the household sector slowed and began to reverse in the years immediately prior to the financial crisis, and this was greatly exacerbated during the crisis years by the loss of job opportunities for those in the lower portions of the income distribution. We show that the distribution of income within the household sector has continued to worsen in the years since the financial crisis and that the deterioration is now evident in both the top and bottom halves of the distribution.

We also find that the standard measures of the Korean income distribution systematically understate the degree of inequality by excluding many households in the top (some of the self-employed) and bottom (the unemployed and retired) portions of the distribution. We use the National Survey of Household Income and Expenditure, which is comprehensive in its coverage but was last undertaken in 2000, to show that the degree of understatement is substantial in the most commonly used reports.[4]

It is also noteworthy that differences in the composition of earners within families have had an important equalizing effect on the distribution

---

4. The problem has been of somewhat diminished importance in recent years, as the Korea National Statistical Office has broadened its basic household survey beyond its original focus on urban wage-earners to include the incomes of a wider range of households.

of household income. Families at the top of the distribution are largely dependent on a single earner, and the situation has changed very little over the years. In contrast, families in the lower portion of the distribution are far more likely to have multiple earners, because of earnings either by the spouse or by employed children. This equalizing role of spousal earnings in Korea is a surprising contrast to the situation in other high-income countries, such as the United States, where a positive correlation of spousal earnings and a shift to two-earner households have contributed to a widening of the distribution of family incomes.

Most of the growing inequality of family incomes over the past decade can be traced to a widening of the distribution of wage incomes. Since the mid-1990s the distribution of earnings has increased at both the top and the bottom of the distribution. In the Household Income and Expenditure Survey (HIES) the deterioration is most pronounced for workers below the median wage, but the situation is less clear cut for the Occupational Wage Survey, which shows a widening of wage differences throughout the distribution.

We also find that large portions of the change in the earnings distribution appear to be related to changes in the returns to education. From 1985 up to the mid-1990s, the wage premium of those with a college degree relative to high school graduates consistently fell, but it has risen during the most recent decade. Similarly the wage discount for those with less than a high school degree narrowed prior to 1995 and has widened dramatically thereafter. Within the HIES data, changes in the returns to education account for nearly the entire decline in wage inequality between 1985 and 1995 and its increase after 1998. However, education factors cannot account for the extraordinary rise of inequality in the midst of the 1998 crisis, which was concentrated in the lower half of the distribution and probably could be traced to the surge of unemployment.

Finally, in Chapter 3 we are surprised to find that Korea has one of the highest incidences of poverty among countries in the Organization for Economic Cooperation and Development (OECD). This is due almost entirely to a very high rate of poverty among the elderly and it reflects the immature nature of the public pension system. The poverty rate among families with children is well below the OECD average.

CAUSES OF INCREASED INEQUALITY

Part II of the study is directed toward examining some of the potential explanations for the observed changes in the income distribution. Chapter 4 relates measures of income inequality to improvements in per capita income in Korea over time, contrasting its experience with the well-known Kuznets hypothesis that posits an inverted-U-shape relationship between inequality and the level of economic development. We find that the Kuznets hypothesis does not apply to the case of Korea, where changes in income levels have had no persistent association with the evolution of income inequality over time, and we examine more recent studies of the relationship between growth and income inequality in Korea. We find some correlation between increased income inequality and other subsidiary variables, such as market openness and population aging. That is, we find that measures of market openness, such as the ratio of private capital flows to GDP, appear to be associated with increased inequality. Furthermore, since the elderly have lower levels of average income than those of working age, an increase in the share of the population that is elderly results in an increase in the poverty rate and a worsening of the income distribution.

At the end of Chapter 4 we adopt a more dynamic approach that examines the change in income inequality in relation to business cycle fluctuations. In the years prior to and including the financial crisis, we can document a strong negative relationship between rates of poverty and economic growth, but there is reduced evidence of a strong relationship in the more recent period. We find that all income classes are affected by business cycle fluctuations, but the impacts tend to be most pronounced for the lower-income groups. Specifically, when nonfarm GDP rises by 1 percent, the income of households in the first income decile increases by 1.6 percent, whereas the income gains of those in the higher deciles vary between 1.2 and 0.8 percent.

Chapter 5 provides a more detailed examination of the potential influence on the income distribution of three factors that have been the focus of the international discussion: changes in demographics, educational attainment, and openness to global markets. The proportion of the population age 65 or older is predicted to double in Korea between 2000 and 2018, a rate far faster than in other OECD countries. Korea also has had one of the world's fastest rates of gain in educational attainment.

We argue that a combination of dramatic changes in the demographic composition and educational attainment of the work force can account for an initial equalizing pattern of change in the income distribution, followed by a pattern of increasing inequality after the mid-1990s. Due to a strong correlation between the changes in educational attainment and age, we use a variety of models to distinguish between the two aspects.

In our analysis of the role of education, we use data on the earnings of male heads of households from the 1985–2008 HIES. Treating education and experience (age) as exogenous determinants of current earnings, we estimate Mincerian regressions in which the log of income is related to five educational categories and ten five-year age categories. We observe that education had an equalizing effect on income during the first half of our period but became a source of increased inequality after the crisis. Similar to our prior results, the coefficients on the age variables yield a strongly humped profile, as average earnings roughly triple between age 25 and 50, and decline to half their peak at age 60 to 65. Examining both the ratio of earnings at the 90th percentile of the wage distribution to the median, and the ratio of median earnings to earnings at the 10th percentile, we note that the residual inequality, after adjusting for education and age, has remained largely constant over the period. The implication of the analysis is that changes in the structure of education and age—a rise in the proportion of highly skilled workers in the middle age groups and the growing importance of older workers, with their lower earnings—can account for both the initial decline in inequality and its rise in more recent years.

We further explore how each age and education level has contributed to inequality through decomposition analysis. Again, gains in educational attainment are found to have had an equalizing effect in the early part of the period, as increases in the supply of skilled workers contributed to the narrowing of the wage distribution, but it has been a source of increased inequality more recently as the pace of improvements in educational attainment has slowed. The decomposition method highlights the importance of changes in the age distribution of the work force. In particular, the strong role of age in accounting for changes in the wage distribution is the result both of the more steeply humped shape of the age-earnings profile and the steadily rising share of older persons in the work force. The worldwide trend toward a knowledge-based economy will exacerbate the deteriorating position of the aged and uneducated in Korea. As the supply of workers expands in the global market, wages and employment opportunities for workers of low technical ability in Korea will plummet, and the disparities caused by the age and educational composition of the work force will continue to expand.

Chapter 5 concludes with a discussion of other factors and their potential role. Changing domestic policies regarding minimum wage and increased trade owing to the opening of global markets appear to have had little influence on the income distribution. However, we have not fully examined the role of an increased polarization of the labor market between regular workers, who have considerable employment protection and access to a full range of social insurance programs, and the large number of nonregular workers on fixed-length contracts, who have lower wages and limited access to social insurance. Because nonregular workers are not well identified in the household survey, we are not able to separate the effects of employment status from the other influences (education and age) on earnings.

THE ROLE OF THE PUBLIC SECTOR

Part III of our study examines the role of government policies and their effects on the income distribution. Chapter 6 reviews the recent evolution of four major social insurance programs in Korea and assesses the challenges to their future viability. The most striking feature of Korea's social welfare programs is their small scale, and as a whole the system therefore constitutes a relatively weak social safety net for the population. Indeed, compared with similar OECD countries, Korea has the lowest public social-welfare expenditures as a share of GDP. To some degree this is a result of the nascent condition of some programs—such as the national pension system. However, limited coverage and rigid cost controls also limit the magnitude of benefits in areas such as medical care and public assistance. Overall, we find the social programs to be well designed and efficiently managed, but funded on a modest scale.

In addition, two challenges are common to most of the programs we discuss. First, there is a problem of low coverage, particularly with the national pension system and the employment insurance program. Korea incorporates a substantially lower percentage of its population in these programs than the OECD average. The low coverage rate seems to be closely related to the problem of the growing polarization of the labor market between "regular" and "nonregular" workers. A reform of the structures governing the labor market may be a prerequisite to a successful expansion in the coverage of the social insurance programs. Second, a period of extremely rapid population aging will put great strain on the system, as the elderly account for a growing share of the expenditures. Below, we briefly discuss our central findings on each program.

The National Pension Service (NPS) was introduced in 1988, amid a time of transition in living arrangements for the elderly in Korea. In previous decades the elderly relied almost exclusively on intergenerational coresidence, whereas today nearly three-quarters of Korea's elderly citizens live in independent accommodations. The NPS was planned as a funded defined-benefit system, and because it is a new system with few individuals receiving benefits, the reserves of the NPS have expanded dramatically in recent years. However, we identify three central challenges that may lead to solvency issues in the long term. First, rapid population aging—itself a result of a declining birth rate—will exert enormous strains on the funding of the pension system. Second, there is a severe problem of poverty among the elderly in Korea: in 2008, 31 percent of households headed by a person over the age of 65 reported income below the minimum income standard. Third, more than 15 percent of the work force remains outside of the pension program.

Recent long-term projections of the NPS reveal the strains these challenges place on the solvency of the system. The current contribution rate—a percent of payroll—is insufficient to sustain the system on a long-term basis, and it is projected to run out of money by the year 2060, at which time the contribution rate would have to jump from 9 percent to more than 23 percent to maintain promised benefits. Given the speed of the aging of Korea's population, it is vital that the contribution rate be adjusted in the near future to avoid an unsustainable burden on future workers. A fully funded system would require a contribution rate nearly double the current 9 percent.

Korea operates a universal public health care system that combines low public cost with a substantial degree of private payments. Health insurance is provided by a government-run single-payer system, but the provision of health care services is largely private. Similar to the NPS, the national health insurance system has difficulties incorporating the self-employed and irregular workers, but the contribution rate is a fixed percentage of income, with no adjustment for family size. That makes it relatively affordable for low-income families. The overall health care system accounts for a small share of GDP by comparison with other OECD countries, but there are common complaints regarding the limited range of services and high copayments. The Korean government is under considerable pressure to expand the system by reducing the magnitude of the copayments. However, the current system relies on the insured to restrain costs, and a large reduction in the rate of copayment would limit the effectiveness of the cost constraints. Although copayments were changed in 2009 to reflect income levels, they still remain a large burden for the low-income population.

Employment insurance did not cover a meaningful percentage of the population until after the financial crisis of 1997–1998. Historically, the focus in Korea has been on preventing unemployment rather than softening its impact. Coverage continues to be limited, with just over half of wage and salary workers enrolled in 2005, and there are strong restrictions on eligibility for benefits. Nevertheless, the program has made strides in including more of the population and expanding benefits, and it played a much bigger role during the 2008 global financial crisis than in the 1998 Asian financial crisis.

Similar to employment insurance, public welfare assistance is a relatively new program in Korea. The National Basic Livelihood Security System (NLBSS) was established in 2000 to replace an existing, smaller program. Although NBLSS expenditures grew by more than 10 percent annually from 2002 to 2007, the current total remains equal to only 0.3 percent of GDP. Compared with an OECD average of roughly 6 percent of GDP, spending on public assistance is the area of greatest divergence between Korea and comparator countries in regard to social insurance programs.

Chapter 7 takes a detailed look at the tax system in Korea to evaluate its role in the income distribution. We show that most of the changes in the tax system have had an equalizing effect on the income distribution, but they have been largely offset by the growth of nominal incomes, which pushes taxpayers into higher marginal tax brackets. The Korean income tax is not fully indexed for inflation, and most past analysis does not account for inflation in the evaluation of tax progressivity.

Overall, we find the tax system in Korea to be relatively ineffective in reallocating income to reduce inequality. The Gini coefficient of after-tax income is barely smaller than that of pretax income, primarily because of the large tax-exempt amount in the income tax system. In addition, there is significant tax evasion by the self-employed. Problems of tax exemption and tax evasion will only be exacerbated by the recent extension of national pension system coverage to the self-employed. Since there is a far higher probability among the self-employed of underreported income or other methods of tax evasion, this policy change will worsen horizontal inequities in tax and social insurance contributions. Thus we conclude Chapter 7 by emphasizing the need for tax administration reform as a method to develop a more equitable distribution of resources in Korea. We measure the distributional consequences of the tax and transfer system by comparing measures of inequality before and after accounting for taxes and transfers, and we find that tax and transfer programs have very modest effects on the overall income distribution, with private transfers actually comprising the most redistributive item.

Finally, in Chapter 8, we use various measurements of program efficiency to evaluate the effectiveness of the existing tax and public welfare programs as tools for reducing income inequality and poverty. Most of our analysis suggests that the programs are not well targeted on the population of poor households. We then discuss pre- and postevaluation methods to improve program effectiveness, and we propose some policy measures by which Korea can construct an institutionalized system for evaluating and improving its welfare programs. In general the programs are too limited in scale; Korea needs to expand its spending on basic welfare objectives, particularly those that are directed at the aged.

Implications for Policy

Korea's success in sustaining a high rate of economic growth over a half century while maintaining relatively low levels of income inequality is a remarkable accomplishment. However, in the course of our research we have also been struck by some aspects of the income distribution that differentiate Korea from other relatively advanced economies. By focusing on worker households and excluding single-person households and those with a retired head, many studies have overstated the degree of income equality in Korea and understated the magnitude of the poverty problem.

There has been a substantial worsening of both the income distribution and poverty in the years after the 1997–1998 financial crisis. We argue that this worsening can be traced to a combination of changes in the age distribution and the levels of educational attainment. There is an increasing gap between well-educated young workers and an older population of workers with fewer job skills, who are increasingly likely to be retired or unemployed. The skill distinctions are intensified by the increasing duality of the labor market, split between a middle-aged, skilled work force in regular employment and older and less-skilled workers with irregular employment in an informal sector of small enterprises. Korea's poverty problem is severe but extremely concentrated among the elderly. We suggest that Korea could best address these problems with reforms that would reduce the duality of the labor market and increase the magnitude of income support for those of retirement age. It needs to change incentives under which firms dismiss older workers at ages that are well short of full retirement. Also, it should expand job training and retraining programs to improve the employability of older workers.

We also found that the effectiveness of both the Korean welfare system and the tax system is quite low. Accordingly, Korea needs to employ various methods of improving the efficacy of redistributive policies. First, it should expand access to social welfare benefits for workers in irregular employment. Second, it could address the immediate problem of poverty among the elderly by expanding the size of the means-tested basic pension program to supplement the income of those who lack sufficient years of coverage under the national pension system. Third, Korea needs to undertake a restructuring of its income tax system to increase the degree of progressivity. Incomplete indexation for inflation has compressed the tax brackets, and the system suffers from extensive tax avoidance by the self-employed.

PART I
Measuring Income Inequality and Poverty

Korea has achieved remarkable economic success over the past half century. Real income per capita has increased thirteenfold since 1960 (an average annual rate of 5.5 percent), absolute poverty levels have been drastically reduced, and the country has been acclaimed for avoiding the large increases in income inequality that have been so evident in other emerging market economies. This is a remarkable long-term record of shared economic gains. Since the 1997–1998 financial crisis, however, there has been a strengthening of the public's perception of growing inequality. It is often noted that the Koreans exhibit a strong sense of egalitarianism, and the outsider's view, that Korea has relatively favorable income distribution, is not shared within the country (Choo [1993] suggests that the discrepancy may be due to the public's emphasis on wealth—particularly the value of land and housing—in contrast to economists' focus on income).

In the following two chapters, we examine the empirical evidence with respect to changes in the distribution of income and Korea's progress toward reducing poverty. Chapter 2 is devoted largely to the question of the degree of income inequality at the household level and the extent of change over the past quarter century. The chapter also provides a discussion of the available data sources for household incomes: specifically, the coverage and shortcomings of the various surveys. Chapter 3 is more narrowly focused on the measurement of poverty, its change over time, and its distribution among various socioeconomic groups.

CHAPTER 2

Trends in Korean Income Inequality

In this chapter we review the evidence with regard to recent changes in the distribution of income in Korea. While we shall report on some of the studies of the income distribution extending back over the past four decades, the focus is on the years since Korea's conversion to a democratic government in 1987, a period that includes the years preceding the financial crisis, the crisis years, and the subsequent period of economic recovery. With the onset of the financial crisis, the Korean economy experienced an extraordinary shock: the country suffered an abrupt and severe reduction in aggregate incomes—a fall in national income of more than 10 percent. How were the costs of the crisis distributed among the population, and who gained the most during the recovery? The question of the equitable distribution of gains from Korea's growth in the recovery is controversial, in part because the nation lacks comprehensive survey evidence on the pattern of change in household incomes over the past several decades. Thus, much of the argument about the extent to which income inequality is a growing problem results from disagreement over how to assemble the evidence from a set of incomplete surveys.

In the following section we look first at research evidence on the long-term trends in the income distribution dating back to the mid-1960s. The period from 1960 up to the transition to full democracy also marks Korea's growth from its former position among the world's poorer countries to middle-income status. The period is marked, however, by a severe shortage of comprehensive data on the income distribution, and the data issues have been extensively evaluated in prior studies. In subsequent sections, our focus is on the more recent developments, with a particular emphasis on the pattern of change in the years after the financial crisis. We begin that discussion with a review of the macroeconomic evidence concerning the extent to which workers and households have shared in the growth of the Korean economy since the crisis. Has the disposable income of the household sector risen in line with growth in the total economy, or is a larger proportion being diverted into the incomes of corporations and the government? The remaining sections of the chapter are more microeconomic in their use of survey data to examine trends in the distribution of incomes within the household sector. We outline the characteristics of the various sources of data and the conclusions of previous empirical studies, and present some of our own evidence and interpretation.

Income Distribution in the Pre-democratization Era

The year 1987 certainly represents a major turning point in the political history of Korea, but it is also alleged that it marks a significant shift in the pattern of change in the income distribution. As mentioned above, however, the evidence on the distribution of incomes in earlier decades is very limited. Surveys of urban household incomes and consumption began to be produced on an annual basis in the 1960s with early versions of what is now the Household Income and Expenditure Survey (HIES). However, those surveys were limited to urban households of two or more persons and collected income information only for the households whose head was a wage earner, excluding those without employment and the self-employed. In contrast, information on consumption was collected from all of the surveyed households. A similar survey was undertaken for farm and fishery households, but other households in rural areas were not included. Kookshin Ahn (1997) reports that 40 percent of all households were excluded from the income portion of the two surveys in 1980, and prior to 1977, the HIES excluded many high-income households. The primary method used to fill in the gaps has been to compare consumption data between wage-earner households and other household types to infer levels of income for the non-wage-earner households, and to make a variety of other adjustments to correct for various shortcomings of the survey data.

There are three primary reports on the distribution of income at the level of all Korean households that extend back to the early 1980s and prior

Table 2.1. Alternative Estimates of the Gini Coefficient of Inequality, 1965–2000

	Choo	*Social Statistics Survey*	*Ahn*
1965	0.344	—	0.337
1970	0.332	—	0.313
1976	0.391	—	0.390
1980	—	0.389	0.357
1982	0.357	—	0.377
1985	—	0.345	0.380
1986	0.337	—	0.377
1988	—	0.336	0.384
1990	0.323	—	0.402
1993	—	0.310	0.380

Source: Choo (1993), Korea National Statistical Office (1988, 1997), and K. Ahn (1997).

decades: (1) a series of studies by Choo (1982, 1993) undertaken with various associates; (2) periodic Social Statistics Surveys from the National Statistical Office; and (3) estimates from Ahn and Kim (1987) and K. Ahn (1997).[1] Choo and his associates produced estimates of the income distribution back to 1965 by combining information on farm and nonfarm families, using relative consumption data to infer the level of income of nonworker households, and adjusting the survey results for the underreporting of high-income families. Ahn used different methods to estimate the incomes of urban nonworker households and obtained divergent results for the post-1976 period. All of these studies focused on the Gini coefficient as their primary measure of the income distribution.[2]

As shown in Table 2.1, the combination of the estimates of Choo and the Social Statistics Survey suggests that the income distribution widened between 1965 and 1976 but then entered a long period of sustained narrowing that continued right up to the early 1990s. K. Ahn reports a similar pattern of deterioration in the years prior to 1976, but he argues

---

1. A more complete set of references, with a discussion, is provided in K. Ahn (1997).

2. The Gini coefficient is a measure of inequality that ranges between zero (everyone has the same income) and unity (one person has all of the income).

that the subsequent narrowing of the distribution stopped in 1982 and that the estimated Gini coefficient remained largely unchanged throughout the 1980s.

It is difficult to determine which version of the historical record is correct. The differences are concentrated in the estimates for nonfarm households, since Ahn reports even larger declines in inequality among farm households. Within the nonfarm sector, the Choo and Ahn studies use the same data source for the income of urban worker households, and the divergences can be traced to different methods of imputing the income of nonworker households from the consumption data. Consumption is known to be an unreliable proxy for income, and there is no good way to construct the required income data in the absence of direct surveys—particularly for households such as those of the self-employed and unemployed, which are likely to differ in major respects from worker households. There is only limited public evaluation of the Social Statistics Surveys, which were based on reported incomes, but K. Ahn (1997, 40) reports significant variation in the types of households that were included in successive surveys. Finally, the estimates from these three sources do not imply a particularly low level of income inequality in the 1980s in comparison with other countries. The measures of the Gini coefficient are well below those of the United States, but they are close to the average of the OECD countries. However, as we discuss more fully later in the book, international comparisons are often quite tenuous because other countries have similar variations in the types of households that are included in the surveys.

A Macroeconomic Perspective

A substantial portion of the current concern about the distribution of gains from economic growth can be traced to a surprisingly large decline in the household share of national income over the past decade. This is most evident in the part A of Figure 2.1, which reports the share of gross national income (GNI) received by households on a before- and after-tax basis for the years 1985 to 2008. In the years prior to the financial crisis, before-tax household incomes varied within a narrow range of 77 percent to 80 percent of GNI. This share shot up to 83 percent in the worst year of the crisis but then fell to a low of 71 percent by 2002. It has remained near that level in recent years. On an after-tax basis, the decline has been even more striking: a household share of only 59 percent in 2008, compared with a pre-crisis average of 69 percent. Thus, while the growth rate of the overall economy may have largely recovered from the crisis, the incomes of households continue to grow much more slowly (Figure 2.1B).

Some details of the realignment of incomes are given in Table 2.2. To begin with, much of the shift in income shares is related to a rise in

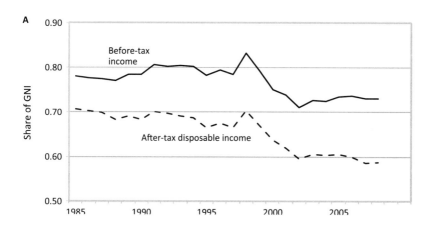

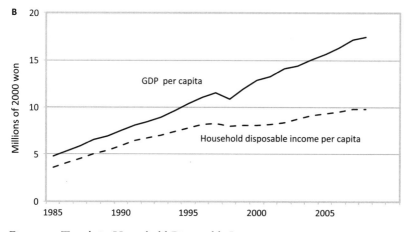

Figure 2.1. Trends in Household Disposable Income, 1985–2008
(*A*) Household income share of gross national income. (*B*) Income per capita (constant prices).
Source: Based on data from national accounts (Bank of Korea 2010), "Income by Institutional Sector" table.

Table 2.2. Distribution of Gross National Income by Institution, 1988–2008 (percent of gross national income)

	Government primary income (1)	Corporate primary income (2)	Household primary income		
			Total (3)	Labor compensation (4)	Business and property income (5)
1988–1992	12.5	16.1	71.8	44.5	27.3
1993–1997	13.4	15.4	71.6	46.6	24.9
1998	14.0	12.8	73.7	45.2	28.6
1999	14.3	15.4	70.3	43.6	26.7
2000	14.8	16.5	68.7	43.2	25.5
2001	14.8	17.7	67.5	43.8	23.7
2002	15.0	20.0	65.0	43.4	21.6
2003	14.7	19.2	66.1	44.5	21.6
2004	14.1	20.3	65.6	44.6	21.1
2005	14.2	19.8	65.9	45.9	20.0
2006	14.8	19.2	65.9	46.2	19.8
2007	15.2	20.2	64.6	46.0	18.6
2008	15.2	21.6	63.2	45.7	17.5
1988–1997	12.1	15.9	72.0	45.0	27.0
1998–2000	13.9	15.2	71.0	45.5	25.5
2001–2008	14.7	19.8	65.5	45.0	20.5

Source: Consolidated National Accounts (Bank of Korea 2010) and authors' calculations.

the corporate share, as enterprises increased their profit margins and retained large portions of the gains rather than raising dividend payments.[3] The corporate share of primary incomes rose from an average of 16 percent of GNI in the five years prior to the crisis to a peak of 22 percent by 2008 (Table 2.2, column 2).[4] There was also a small increase

---

3. This rise in the corporate profit rate over the past decade is not limited to Korea. It is particularly marked in countries as diverse as the United States, Japan, and China.

4. "Primary income" is the term used in the national accounts to indicate the income received from current production, prior to any redistribution through taxes and transfers.

in the government share. As a result, the household share of primary incomes fell from a pre-crisis average of 72 percent to a low of 63 percent in 2008.

Normally, we would expect the rise in the corporate (profit) share to be reflected in a decline in the portion of income going to labor compensation. Within the household sector, however, the changes are more complex because a large portion of the Korean economy is devoted to self-employment in small businesses, where the share of income has been steadily declining as the work force has shifted from self-employment to wage and salary jobs. As shown in column 5 of Table 2.2, the decline in business and property incomes has been particularly rapid in recent years, but with less evidence of a compensatory rise in wage payments. Overall, larger portions of the nation's income are being retained as saving within the business sector and in the form of government budget surpluses. In a sense, those incomes still accrue to households, as owners of the corporations, and much of the government surplus is concentrated in the public pension accounts, which will ultimately be paid to individuals. However, those implicit payments are not obvious to households that focus on cash flows, and they will not be captured in surveys of household incomes.

Finally, changes in the pattern of price changes have put additional pressures on households' economic welfare. In recent years, the prices of the consumption items that households buy have been increasing more rapidly than the prices of the products that they produce. That is, households have been suffering from a persistent loss in their terms of trade. The historical pattern of change is shown in Figure 2.2 for the period from 1980 to 2008. If we measure the price of the products they buy with the personal consumption expenditure (PCE) price deflator of the national accounts, and the output prices of the products they produce with the overall GDP deflator, consumers have experienced an erosion of their standard of living of 12 percent since 1997, simply from a decline in their terms of trade. That translates into an average annual loss of about 1 percent per year. This is in addition to the decline in the household share of nominal incomes. The fall in the terms of trade first emerged in the mid-1990s, and it stands in sharp contrast to the pattern of change in the 1980s, when households actually had terms-of-trade gains that augmented their real income growth by more than 1 percent per year. The decline is roughly consistent with the fall in Korea's external

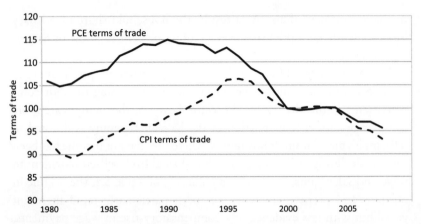

Figure 2.2. Alternative Measures of Terms of Trade for Korean Workers, 1980–2008
Worker terms of trade is the price of the products workers consume relative to the price of the products they produce. The price of products that workers produce is measured by the GDP price deflator, and the price of the products that they consume is measured by either the consumer price index (CPI) or the personal consumption expenditure (PCE) price deflator for private consumption in the national accounts. Index: year 2000 = 100. *Source:* Computed with data from Bank of Korea (2010) and Korea National Statistical Office (2010).

terms of trade (export prices/import prices), and it may reflect the deterioration in the real exchange rate in the aftermath of the financial crisis. Higher import prices would raise consumer prices while having no direct effect on the GDP price deflator.

The figure also highlights a large discrepancy between the consumer price index (CPI) and the PCE price deflator of the national accounts as alternative measures of price inflation during the 1990s. The terms of trade as measured by the CPI shows a much larger reversal in Figure 2.2 between the 1980s and the post-crisis years. During the 1990s, the CPI rose at a 5 percent annual rate, compared with almost 7 percent for the PCE price deflator, yet they have increased at nearly identical rates since 2000. In concept, the two indexes measure prices of very similar market baskets, and the large discrepancies are very puzzling. Most macroeconomic analysis is based on the price deflators of the national accounts, but nearly all of the microeconomic analyses of survey data use the CPI. The use of the CPI in the micro studies translates into much higher rates of real income growth during the 1990s. To maximize the comparability between the macro- and microeconomic analysis, we have used the PCE price deflator of the national accounts throughout this study.[5]

As a result of these shifts at the level of the macroeconomic economy, the average household has not experienced much of a recovery from the financial crisis, and measured income growth continues to be much reduced relative to the experience of the years prior to 1998. For example, based on the GDP deflator, per capita real GDP (shown in Figure 2.1B) has been advancing at 4.2 percent per year since 2000, compared with a rate of about 6.4 percent in the ten years ending in 1997. That is, the long-run potential growth rate appears to have slowed by about 2 percent annually. For households, however, the growth of real per capita disposable incomes has slowed from a rate of 5.7 percent per year in the pre-crisis period to a current rate of only 1.3 percent: a much larger slowdown of over 4 percent per year, and a current rate of gain that is less than one-third that of the overall economy. From this perspective, the discontent so evident in the public-opinion polls should not come as a surprise, and the growing gap between the continued expansion of GDP per capita and the near stagnation of household incomes is quite extraordinary. It fuels the perception that households have not benefited to the same extent as businesses from the economic recovery.

Microeconomic Measures of the Income Distribution

The deterioration in the relative position of households that is so evident in the aggregate data can go a long way toward explaining the growing disenchantment with the performance of the economy. However, there are also concerns about widening disparities among individual households, and a belief that the gap between the rich and the poor has increased over time.

Ideally, studies of the income distribution would be based on comprehensive surveys of the total population, and if not conducted on an annual basis, they would follow a regular multiyear cycle. There has been,

---

5. In part, we justify our decision by the broader concept of consumption expenditures employed in the national accounts and because the price deflator uses the components of the CPI as major data sources. Our efforts to obtain an explanation from the Korea National Statistical Office for the discrepancies between the two measures of price change were unsuccessful.

however, no consistent comprehensive survey of the incomes of Korean households. The HIES is the most commonly used source of data at the level of individual households, but for most of the survey's history the income data have been limited to urban wage-earner households with more than two members. The National Survey of Household Income and Expenditure (NSHIE), a large, comprehensive survey of all households, was conducted in 1991, 1996, and 2000. However, it has been discontinued, and the recent focus has been on an expansion in the coverage of the HIES. In addition, the Ministry of Labor conducts an annual survey of enterprises, called the Occupational Wage Survey (OWS), that collects information on the wages, education, gender, and job tenure of employees.

PREVIOUS STUDIES

Korean researchers have made use of all three of the above surveys to investigate changes in the distribution of household income and labor earnings over time and the role of various socioeconomic factors in determining its structure.[6] There is substantial consensus about the general pattern of change over the past two decades.

All-Household Surveys   Hyun and Lim (2002) reported on results from the 1991 and 1996 versions of the NSHIE, which recorded incomes for all household types. They find an increase in overall inequality between the two years for a measure of before-tax market incomes that excludes transfers: an increase in the Gini coefficient from 0.38 to 0.39. However, on an after-tax basis and with the inclusion of transfers, inequality was slightly reduced, reflected in a drop in the Gini coefficient from 0.36 to 0.34. They also experimented with a range of adjustments for changes in family size and found that they had little influence on the conclusions. In a second study (Hyun and Lim 2005), they extended their analysis to include the 2000 survey. Using a slightly different definition of before-tax income than they used in 2002, they found a substantial increase in inequality between 1996 and 2000: the Gini coefficient rose

---

6. Our summary of the existing literature is somewhat distorted by a strong emphasis on articles published in English, but many of the major researchers have published their results in both English and Korean.

from 0.34 to 0.40. They also report a major widening of the distribution: the percent of households with income below 50 percent of the median income rose from 14 percent in 1996 to 19 percent in 2000, and those with incomes above 150 percent of the median rose from 20 percent to 24 percent. On an after-tax basis, the Gini coefficient rose from 0.32 in 1996 to 0.38 in 2000.

Gyu-Jin Hwang (2004) used data from the 1991, 1996, and 2000 NSHIEs to examine the influence of the social insurance programs on the income distribution. He did not report formal measures of inequality and excluded one-person households, but it is clear from the decile distributions that the inequality of before-tax incomes widened substantially between 1996 and 2000. The share of overall income declined for the lowest eight deciles, and the share going to the top decile rose by 5 percentage points. He also argues that, despite large growth in the size of the direct transfer programs and social insurance contributions, they have had a small effect on inequality because the distribution of these payments is very similar to that of before-tax incomes.

Urban Worker Households   By far the most common studies of the income distribution have focused on urban families headed by a wage earner. The analysis is driven by the availability of a long time series for the HIES. Unfortunately, the HIES excludes some of the most critical groups, such as the self-employed, unemployed, and retired.

A recent study by Kwack and Lee (2007) assembled the standard HIES data for 1965 to 2005 and constructed a number of alternative measures of income inequality at the household level. Excluding a discontinuity in the data in 1976–1977, they report that the standard measures of inequality show some decline in the 1960s and 1970s and stable or slightly declining inequality in the 1980s, before they resume a more rapid decline until the financial crisis of 1997–1998. The crisis initiated a sharp rise in inequality, and the situation has remained roughly unchanged in recent years.[7] They also examine the evidence of polarization of the income distribution: the movement of households from the

---

7. The Gini coefficient fell from 0.32 in 1977 to 0.28 in 1997, before jumping back up to 0.32 in 1999. It was 0.31 in 2005. Similarly, the ratio of income earned by the top 10 percent of households to the income earned by the bottom 10 percent fell from 8.8 in 1976 to 7.0 in 1997 before rising to 9.4 in 1998.

middle of the distribution to the two tails. The pattern of change in the measures of polarization has been very similar to that of variations in overall inequality.

Kyungsoo Choi (2003) analyzed the same HIES data for 1982 to 2002 and emphasized the importance of the narrowing gap among educational groups in accounting for the decline in inequality in the late 1980s and early 1990s. However, the among-group differences remained relatively constant over the last half of the sample period and the increase in inequality was largely concentrated within the various educational groups. Choi also argues that this widening of the within-group distribution after the crisis has been particularly pronounced among the least educated, and that this could be traced to a reduction in hours rather than wage rates.

Chulhee Lee (2002) matched the HIES to the Survey of the Economically Active Population—the larger survey of which the HIES is a subsample—for the years 1988, 1993, and 1999. The match provided information on employment and hours of work for household heads and spouses in the household survey. In this way, Lee could decompose changes in household incomes into the contribution of labor and nonlabor income, and the labor income changes could be further separated into the contribution of changes in hours of work and the wage rate. He concluded that reduced inequality of the hourly wage rates of household heads was the dominant source of a substantial narrowing in the distribution of household incomes between 1988 and 1993. In contrast, the 1993–1999 deterioration in the income distribution was the result of many factors in addition to changes in wage rates—such as reduced hours for low-wage households and a relative decline in nonwage incomes. The widening of incomes was concentrated among low-income households, which lost ground relative to the average.

Employer Wage Survey   Another micro-level survey, the Occupational Wage Survey (OWS), collects information from a survey of enterprises and has been the basic data source for several important studies of the wage distribution. Kim and Topel (1995) reported a continuous decline in wage inequality, as measured by the ratio of men's wages at the 90th percentile to wages at the 10th percentile for 1971 to 1989. They attribute the decline to large reductions in the wage premiums for workers with different levels of educational attainment, which could be traced, in turn, to a rapid expansion of the supply of high school and college graduates. Fields and Yoo (2000) also attributed the decline in wage inequality among men to a fall in the return to education. They found that inequality was not reduced among female workers, however. Kang and Yun (2003) extended the analysis to 2000, and reported that the long, steady reduction in wage inequality appears to have come to an end about 1994 and increased in subsequent years. Their analysis suggests that the major factor was a stabilization of the returns to education after 1994.

MEASURING INEQUALITY

We have access to the historical micro-level data of three major surveys: the NSHIE for 1996 and 2000, the HIES for 1985 to 2008, and the OWS for 1985 to 2008. Each of these surveys has problems of frequency or coverage, but together they permit an examination of recent trends in the income distribution from a variety of perspectives, including the magnitude of the income gaps among individuals and households at the top, middle, and bottom of the distribution, changes in the age-income profile, and differences in earnings by gender and level of skill or educational attainment.

We begin with the broadest household survey, the NSHIE, because it allows us to benchmark the income estimates reported in the surveys in terms of the aggregates reported in the national accounts. The benchmarks are useful for ensuring that the surveys capture the macroeconomic phenomena shown in the national accounts. Even though no new wave of the NSHIE is available for the years after 2000, the survey is the only source of information on the components of income for households that are not headed by a wage earner. The HIES has been broadened to include rural households (2003) and single-person households (2006), and for the recent years we have had access to an expanded version of the survey that provides estimates of total income, but not its composition, for households without a wage-earner head.

NSHIE A simple comparison of income by major source for the National Survey of Household Income and Expenditure and the national accounts is shown in Table 2.3. The estimates from the survey are translated into aggregates by multiplying them by the number of households

Table 2.3. Comparison of Incomes in the NSHIE and the National Accounts, 1996 and 2000 (trillions of won)

	1996		2000	
	National accounts	NSHIE	National accounts	NSHIE
Labor income	190.3	185.1	220.7	192.3
Wages and salaries less employees' social contributions	181.4	—	209.4	—
Business income[a]	72.9	93.6	94.3	107.7
Property income	43.7	15.7	60.5	19.1
Interest and dividends	42.5	7.3	59.1	9.9
Rent	1.1	8.4	1.5	9.2
Social benefits	27.3	15.4	34.3	23.1
Pension allowance	—	1.9	—	3.8
Public subsidies	—	0.5	—	2.4
Private subsidies	—	13.0	—	16.9
Total income	334.2	309.9	409.9	342.2

Source: Korea National Income Accounts (Bank of Korea 2010); National Survey of Household Income and Expenditure (Korea National Statistical Office 2002).

[a] The national accounts measure for business income equals the operating surplus of individuals plus withdrawals from income of quasi corporations within income accounts by institutionalized sector. A significant portion of rental income is recorded as business income in the national accounts.

in the survey year.[8] At the aggregate level, the survey appears to capture between 83 percent (2000) and 93 percent (1996) of the household income shown in the national accounts. For the components, the match is very good in 1996 for wage income, and the survey estimate of business income actually exceeds that of the national accounts. On the other hand, the estimates of property income and transfers are very low compared with those of the national accounts. The low reported level of interest and dividend income in the surveys is typical, both because people are reluctant to report such income and because the national accounts include payments to pension accounts and trusts for which individuals

8. The 2000 census counted 14.3 million households, but the NSHIE does not report the incomes of about 1.3 million farm and fishery households.

may not know the details of source income. The match for transfers is worse than it appears because a major component, private transfers, is largely reflective of payments between families and would not be included in the national accounts measure of household income. Overall, there is also some evidence of deterioration in the survey measures of income between 1996 and 2000 because the values fall as a share of the corresponding income from the national accounts.

The major advantage of the NSHIE is that it can be used to measure the change in the income distribution for an inclusive definition of households over the period that encompasses the financial crisis. The major components of household income are reported in Table 2.4. In addition, we include a measure in which the NSHIE estimates are restricted to match the group of households covered by the HIES—excluding non-wage households, one-person households, and those located in rural areas. Average incomes are similar for the broad and narrow definitions of

Table 2.4. Average Income by Source: NSHIE and HIES, 1996 and 2000 (thousands of won)

	1996			2000		
	NSHIE	NSHIE-restricted	HIES	NSHIE	NSHIE-restricted	HIES
Total income	1,993	2,093	2,153	2,185	2,385	2,387
Earnings	1,191	1,876	1,838	1,244	2,108	2,008
Earnings, household head	913	1,496	1,478	896	1,659	1,639
Earnings, spouse	138	207	193	162	250	202
Earnings, others	140	173	167	187	199	167
Business income	592	80	73	666	101	94
Returns from assets	101	72	52	124	98	45
Transfer income	99	53	54	147	73	66
Other income	—	—	—	4	5	173

Source: Author's calculations based on micro-data files from the National Survey of Household Income and Expenditure (Korea National Statistical Office 2002) and the Household Income and Expenditure Survey (Korea National Statistical Office 2009).
Note: "NSHIE-restricted" signifies the NSHIE sample is restricted to urban, wage-earning households of two or more persons.

Table 2.5. Income Inequality Measures: NSHIE and HIES, 1996 and 2000

	Gini	90/10	90/50	50/10
1996				
NSHIE	0.33	4.9	1.9	2.5
NSHIE-restricted	0.26	3.4	1.8	1.9
HIES	0.30	3.9	1.9	2.0
2000				
NSHIE	0.39	7.0	2.2	3.3
NSHIE-restricted	0.30	4.0	1.9	2.1
HIES	0.33	4.2	2.0	2.1

Source: Author's calculations based on micro-data files of NSHIE and HIES (Korea National Statistical Office 2002, 2009).

Note: "NSHIE-restricted" signifies that the NSHIE sample is restricted to urban, wage-earning households of two or more persons.

households because the high average incomes of the self-employed are offset by low incomes among the retired and unemployed households. Second, the NSHIE and HIES estimates of mean incomes for urban wage-earner households were very similar in both 1996 and 2000: thus, the two surveys seem very comparable when they are limited to reporting on identical subpopulations.

Measures of income inequality for the two surveys are also reported in Table 2.5. First, it is clear that a focus on wage-earner households substantially understates the degree of overall income inequality because of the exclusion of nonwage households at both the top and the bottom of the distribution. The Gini coefficient for all households was 0.33 in 1996 compared with 0.26 for the subset of wage-earner households. The Gini coefficient increased substantially between 1996 and 2000 for both household categories, but the increase was particularly large for the broad definition, rising to 0.39. Similar conclusions emerge in a comparison of incomes at the 90th, 50th, and 10th deciles of the income distribution. The 90/10 ratio is 4.9 in 1996 for the broad definition of the NSHIE, rising to 7.0 in 2000. The widening of the income distribution is evident both in the increase in the number of households with very low incomes and those at the top of the distribution. The 90/50 ratio rises from 1.9 to 2.2, but the largest increase in inequality is in the lower portions of the distribution—as seen in the rise in the 50/10 ratio from 2.5 in 1996 to 3.3

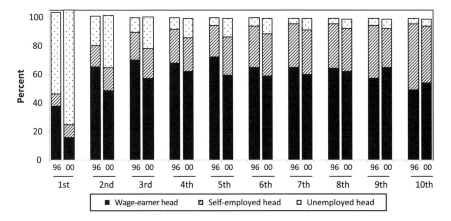

Figure 2.3. Distribution of Households by Type of Household and Income Decile, 1996 and 2000
Source: Computed by the authors from the micro-data files of the NSHIE (Korea National Statistical Office 2002).

in 2000. Increased inequality is also evident for the subset of wage-earner households, but the decile ratios are smaller and the magnitude of change is considerably smaller.

Figure 2.3 further highlights the importance of including non-wage-earner households in the analysis. All of the households in the NSHIE are distributed first by deciles of the income distribution and then by type of household head—wage-earner, self-employed, or not employed. It is evident that wage-earner households are broadly spread across the distribution except in the lowest income decile, which is dominated by households with an unemployed head. In contrast, the self-employed tend to be concentrated in the upper portions of the distribution. Furthermore, there are major changes in the distribution of the three household types between 1996 and 2000. The decline in wage-earner households in the lower quintiles is offset by a rise in the number of unemployed. At the top of the distribution, there is a reduced frequency of self-employed heads of household and a rise in the proportion that are headed by wage earners.

HIES The annual frequency of the HIES does provide an important source of information on changes in the income distribution; nevertheless, as stressed above, for most of its history it provides detailed income data only for households headed by wage earners, failing to take into account

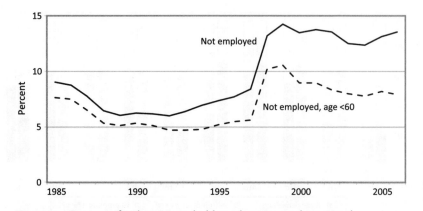

Figure 2.4. Percent of Urban Households with a Nonworking Head, 1985–2006
Survey excludes one-person households. Source: Authors' calculations, based on the micro-data files of the HIES (Korea National Statistical Office 2009).

incomes for important segments of the population. In the survey, the proportion of urban households whose head is a self-employed businessperson—and whose income is thus not reported—has been constant at about 30 percent of the total, but the proportion with a nonworking household head surged in 1998 and has remained at an elevated level in subsequent years (Figure 2.4). To distinguish between those who are probably retired versus the unemployed, the figure also shows the proportion who were not working and below the age of 60. The proportion of urban households with a nonworking head below age 60 rose from 5.6 to 10.2 percent in 1998. While the proportion has declined in subsequent years, it remains around 8 percent through 2006.[9] Clearly, both the retired and the unemployed have grown in importance. Unfortunately, we lack information on the incomes of these other households; in the remainder of this section we focus on the incomes of households headed by a wage earner.[10]

---

9. In the latest surveys examined, from 2007 and 2008, it is not possible to distinguish between the unemployed and the self-employed; therefore we were not able to see what has happened to the proportion of those not employed since 2006.

10. To maintain continuity, rural and single-person households are excluded from the time-series analysis.

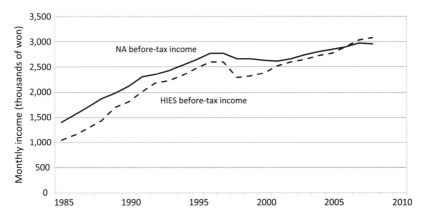

Figure 2.5. Disposable Household Income according to National Accounts and the HIES, 1985–2008

National accounts (NA) and Household Income and Expenditure Survey (HIES) income measures are both converted to 2000 prices with the personal consumption expenditure deflator of the national accounts. The number of households is interpolated from quinquennial census data of the Korea National Statistical Office. *Source:* Constructed by the authors from the micro-data files of the HIES (Korea National Statistical Office 2009) and national accounts (Bank of Korea 2010).

Figure 2.5 compares the estimate of mean income of wage-earner households in the HIES to a national accounts measure based on dividing before-tax incomes by the total number of households for the period 1985 to 2008. The HIES indicates a substantially faster growth of incomes prior to the financial crisis, a very large drop in 1998 that is not as evident in the national accounts' measures of household income, and a more rapid rate of income growth after 2000. There are substantial differences in coverage, and the incomes of urban worker households may be growing somewhat faster than the national average of all households, but the size of the discrepancy in 1998–2000 is troubling.[11] The 1998 decline in the HIES is concentrated in labor income and it is larger, in percentage terms, for the wage income of the spouse and other family members. Part of the problem is that the individual (household) sector of the national accounts shows an offsetting sharp rise in self-employment

---

11. It is also possible that the large decline in average household income between 1997 and 1998 is a result of the change in the HIES sample frame between those two years, but similar breaks are not evident in other transition years.

and property income that offsets some of the decline in wage incomes, but these income sources are underreported in the HIES.

Two summary measures of changes in the income distribution of wage-earner households using the HIES are shown in Figure 2.6A. The Gini coefficient indicates a substantial decline in inequality extending from the 1980s up to the early 1990s, and it appears to level out several years prior to the financial crisis. There is a very sharp rise in the Gini coefficient during the crisis, and it basically remains at that plateau in subsequent years. Judged by this measure, inequality has returned to the levels of the mid-1980s. Over the same period, average family size has steadily declined—from an average of 4.2 members per household in 1985 to 3.26 in 2008—but a scale adjustment for household size has very little effect on the pattern of change.[12] The alternative measure, the ratio of income at the 90th percentile to income at the 10th percentile, behaves similarly to the Gini coefficient. It is more definite in showing that the pattern of declining inequality ended well before the financial crisis and was increasing in the immediate pre-crisis years. It also differs in suggesting that inequality has continued to widen in the years after the crisis, with a pronounced upward jump in 2004 that raises the estimate of inequality well above that of the 1980s.

Figure 2.6B illustrates a separation of the 90/10 decile ratio into measures for the top and bottom halves of the income distribution. The interesting element is that the decline in overall inequality between 1985 and 1993 was concentrated in the upper portions of the distribution where the 90/50 ratio fell from 2.1 to 1.9 compared with largely constant values for the 50/10 ratio. In contrast, the rise in inequality after 1993 has been largely a result of growing income differences in the bottom portions of the distribution as the poor have lost ground relative to middle-income households. There has been very little change in the top half of the distribution.[13] In addition, the change in the 50/10 income ratio is undoubtedly a severe understatement of the widening of the income

---

12. The measure of equivalized income is computed by dividing the household income by the square root of household size. Other formulas for the scale adjustment had no significant influence on the conclusions.

13. In logarithms, the change in the 90/50 ratio between 1985 and 1993 was −10 points, and the change in the 50/10 ratio was −4 points. Between 1993 and 2008 the corresponding changes were +3 and +20 points, respectively.

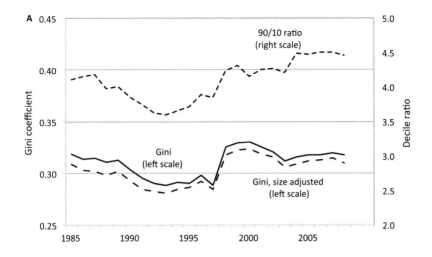

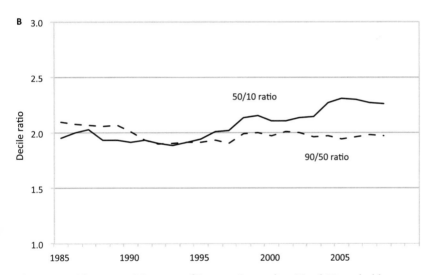

Figure 2.6. Alternative Measures of Income Inequality, Total Household
Income, 1985–2008

(*A*) Gini coefficient and ratio of earnings in 90th decile to 10th decile. (*B*) Ratio of earnings in
90th decile to 50th decile, and earnings in 50th decile to earnings in the 10th. The adjustment
for household size is the number of household members raised to the 0.5 power. *Source:* Authors' estimates, based on the micro-data files of the HIES (Korea National Statistical Office
2009).

distribution at the bottom of the distribution, because the survey excludes the income of the unemployed.

The extent of the rise in income inequality is also affected in important ways by family structures. Thus, it matters greatly whether the issue of income inequality is raised within the context of individual earners or families. The contribution of other household members' income is highlighted in Table 2.6. The top rows show mean earnings for the top and bottom quintiles in the distribution of the wage income of male household heads, measured as a proportion of the overall mean wage in the specific year.[14] For example, males in the bottom quintile had earnings equivalent to 39 percent of mean earnings in 1985, and their relative position rose to 44 percent in 1995, before falling to a low of 34 percent by 2008. Meanwhile, the earnings of men in the top quintile declined from an average wage of 1.99 times the mean to 1.86 in 1995, before rising back up to 1.95 by 2008.

The second section of Table 2.6 reports the average spousal income of those same households. Measured as a proportion of the head's income, spousal earnings are three to four times more important in the bottom quintile than in the top quintile, and the relationship has been quite stable since the mid-1990s. The same calculation is reported in the third section for other earners in the family—three-quarters of whom are children. Here the distribution is even more skewed, as their earnings are a far more significant source of family income for the bottom quintile than for those at the top of the distribution. The fourth section shows the importance of other family income, which consists largely of transfer payments. Again the difference across quintiles of the distribution is very large, and transfers are more important for families at the bottom of the distribution.

Finally, the last section shows total family income, but it maintains the quintile division by the labor income of the household head. It is evident that families in the bottom quintile have raised their relative position by a significant amount relative to the position of the household head alone. In 2008, the family income is 54 percent of the average of all male-headed households, compared with 34 percent for the male head alone. The contribution of other family members' incomes, however, does

---

14. We simplified Table 2.6 by excluding the middle quintiles in the distribution; this has no effect on the conclusions.

Table 2.6. Percent of Average Male-Head Labor Income, by Income Source in the HIES, 1985–2008

	1985	1995	2000	2008
Labor income of household head (multiple of overall mean)				
Quintile 1	0.39	0.43	0.36	0.34
Quintile 5	1.99	1.86	1.92	1.95
Contribution of				
Spouse's labor income (multiple of head's income)				
Quintile 1	0.16	0.31	0.30	0.35
Quintile 5	0.04	0.08	0.08	0.10
Other family members' labor income (multiple of head's income)				
Quintile 1	0.20	0.34	0.41	0.39
Quintile 5	0.02	0.03	0.03	0.03
Nonlabor income (multiple of head's income)				
Quintile 1	0.21	0.30	0.41	0.31
Quintile 5	0.05	0.06	0.05	0.02
Household total income (multiple of overall mean)				
Quintile 1	0.52	0.63	0.58	0.54
Quintile 5	1.86	1.65	1.70	1.72

Source: Authors' calculation from micro-data files of the HIES (Korea National Statistical Office 2009).

Note: The quintile classifications are based solely on the labor income of the household head.

not significantly alter the pattern of a widening of the distribution of family incomes between 1995 and 2008.

The distinction between the dominant role of the head's earnings at the top of the income distribution and the contribution of other members at the bottom is a striking feature of the income distribution in Korea. In 2008, in the top quintile, 67 percent of male heads are the sole earner, compared with only 49 percent in the bottom quintile. In addition, the equalizing role of spousal earnings is in sharp contrast with countries, such as the United States, where the increased labor-force participation of married women has led to growing family inequality because of a strong positive correlation of spouses' incomes, or assortative mating (Burtless 1999). In Korea, the relative income contribution of married women declines with income, despite the fact that husbands and wives have nearly identical education levels that increase in step with family income. In addition, we do not find a significant difference in the wife's relative contribution for families with and without children, implying that the differences cannot be attributed to the costs of child-rearing or to a lack of access to day-care facilities. Cameron, Dowling, and Worswick (2001) find that the weak correlation between women's education and labor force participation also differentiated Korea from other Asian countries. They attributed it to cultural factors that led to strongly defined gender roles in Korea compared with other countries.

Another surprising aspect is the very low percentage of house-holds—3.7 percent in 2008—that have income both from the spouse and from other members. Working spouses leave the labor force at a very young age, on average near 40, and the other working family members are largely adult children in families where the spouse is near age 50. Since 2003, the National Statistical Office has released an expanded version of the HIES that includes the total income of nonearner households, and it extended the scope to include rural households in 2003 and one-person households in 2006.[15] Thus, the survey has been enlarged to represent the full population. Measures of income inequality based on the expanded data files are reported in Table 2.7. They further highlight the conclusion from the discussion of the NSHIE that the standard measures of income distribution, based on the incomes of urban wage-earner households, severely understate the degree of income inequality in Korea. In 2006, for example, the 90/10 ratio increases from 4.5 for wage-earner households with two or more members to 5.8 for all urban households with two or more members, and to 9.6 with the inclusion of rural and one-person households. The increase in the scope of the household coverage has a less dramatic effect on the Gini coefficient. In 2006 it rises from 0.317 for wage-earner households to just 0.352 for ur-ban two-member-plus households and 0.399 for the nationwide sample, because most of the added households are at the extremes of the distri-bution.[16] However, the broader scope does imply that the egalitarian view of Korean society is, at least in the income dimension, exaggerated.

---

15. The term "earner household" refers to a household with a head who is either a wage earner or self-employed. A "nonearner household" has a head who is either un-employed or retired. The data files still exclude the details of income by member and by type of income for nonearner households.

16. The Gini coefficient gives greater weight than the 90/10 ratio to households in the middle of the income distribution.

Table 2.7. Income Inequality Measures for Alternative Subgroups of the HIES, 2004–2008

Measure	2004	2006	2008
Urban wage-earner households			
90/10 ratio	4.5	4.5	4.5
90/50 ratio	2.0	2.0	2.0
50/10 ratio	2.3	2.3	2.3
Gini coefficient	0.316	0.317	0.317
All urban 2+-person households			
90/10 ratio	5.5	5.8	5.9
90/50 ratio	2.0	2.1	2.1
50/10 ratio	2.7	2.8	2.8
Gini coefficient	0.343	0.352	0.355
All households, nationwide			
90/10 ratio	5.9	9.6	10.4
90/50 ratio	2.0	2.2	2.3
50/10 ratio	2.9	4.3	4.6
Gini coefficient	0.351	0.399	0.411

Source: Computed by the authors from the expanded versions of the HIES (Korea National Statistical Office 2009).

Note: All tabulations for urban households (two or more persons) include the income of households with a self-employed or nonearner head. The nationwide sample includes households in rural areas and, for 2006 and later, one-person households.

In addition, the HIES is not particularly suitable for examining the distribution of wages at the level of individual members of the household. Nothing is known about characteristics of the spouse that would influence earnings, such as age and educational attainment, prior to a revision of the survey in 1998. The earnings of other household members are reported only on a combined basis, limiting the analysis to their average earnings. Furthermore, no information is obtained about the hours of work or whether employment is full-time or part-time. Chulhee Lee (2002) developed a means of adding information on hours worked by linking the HIES to the labor force survey for 1993–1999, but we did not have access to a comparable data set. Instead, we have focused on the OWS as an alternative source of information on the distribution of labor income.

OWS The Occupational Wage Survey offers some key advantages for examining the distribution of wages. Most important, it provides data on the earnings of individuals from the perspective of employer, as opposed to the focus on household earnings that underlies the HIES. It is also unusual among business-level surveys in collecting information on important characteristics of individual employees, such as educational attainment, tenure, and gender. Its most significant limitation is that it excludes workers in enterprises with fewer than five employees (or ten, prior to 1999) and large portions of the public sector. Thus, it does not offer a representative sample of all wage earners. The OWS and HIES are particularly different in their industry distributions: workers in manufacturing represent 39 percent of the total number of employed participants in the OWS, compared with 27 percent of those in the HIES. On the other side, 13 percent of the HIES sample is in construction compared with only about 6 percent of those in the OWS. Finally, the work force included in the OWS is significantly younger than the heads of worker households in the HIES. It is also evident that an increasing proportion of workers who do not have a high school degree are excluded from the OWS.

The two surveys yield very similar measures of the general trend for wage increase over the years 1985 to 2008, but the OWS indicates a smaller decline in the crisis years of 1998–1999 and a faster rate of wage increase in recent years. We suspect that this is due to the greater exclusion of part-time and underemployed workers from the OWS, since they are more commonly employed in small firms. A comparison of the measures of wage inequality from the OWS with those discussed earlier for the HIES is shown in Figure 2.7. First, there is a significantly greater degree of wage inequality in the HIES than in the OWS during the 1990s, as shown by the much higher Gini coefficients (Figure 2.7A). However, both surveys report the same general pattern—a decline in wage inequality up to the mid-1990s and a reversal over the past decade—although the cycle is more pronounced in the OWS. Second, the large jump in inequality that is found in the 90/10 ratio for the HIES around the time of the financial crisis is much less evident in the OWS, but the latter indicates a long-term erosion over the full decade that is similar in magnitude to the change in the HIES. The division in the decile ratio between the top and bottom halves of the wage distribution results in very similar estimates of wage inequality at the top of the distribution (Figure 2.7B); the OWS suggests a greater degree of narrowing in the early years and increased inequality more recently. The largest difference results

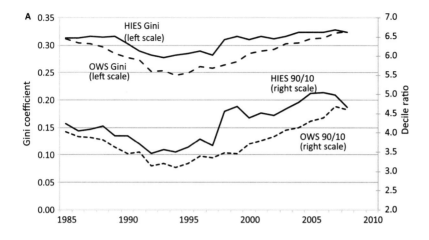

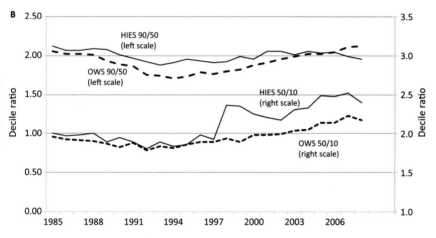

Figure 2.7. Comparison of Earnings Inequality among Men, HIES and OWS, 1985–2008

(*A*) Gini coefficient and 90/10 ratio. (*B*) 90/50 and 90/10 ratios. Data are restricted to male heads of household in the Household Income and Expenditure Survey and male workers in the Occupational Wage Survey. *Source:* Authors' computations, based on the micro-data files of the HIES (Korea National Statistical Office 2009) and OWS (Ministry of Employment and Labor 2009).

from the jump in the 50/10 ratio in 1998–1999 for the HIES data in comparison to the very gradual increase for the OWS, but the OWS shows a continued widening of the 90/50 ratio in recent years, whereas it has narrowed in the HIES.

The discrepancies may reflect the differences in the structure of the two sample populations during periods of sharply changing employment, but there are also other distinctions between the two surveys. The HIES, based on households, includes workers who may have lost or changed their job during the month, whereas the OWS measure is for a specific job. Thus job transitions—particularly from full-time to part-time work—would be much more apparent in the HIES survey. However, job transitions would not seem to account for the continued differences in the years after the crisis. Adjusted for inflation, average wages in the lowest quintile of the HIES fell by 37 percent in 1998 and have never returned to their pre-crisis level. In contrast, the 1997–98 wage changes in the OWS were far smaller and more uniform across the deciles of the distribution. By excluding firms with employment below a minimal size, the OWS may have missed the transition of workers to less-well-paying jobs in retail and similar industries. There has also been considerable discussion of the rapid growth of the proportion of workers in nonstandard employment arrangements (J. Ahn 2004). These workers may also be underrepresented in the OWS. The potential influence of changes in the structure of employment on the wage distribution will be examined in more detail in a later chapter.

ROLE OF EDUCATION

Korea is widely cited for the extent to which it has raised the educational attainment of its work force. Over the period from 1985 to 2006, the average number of years of schooling for workers age 25 to 45 has increased from 11.5 to 14.[17] Those changes in educational attainment can have important effects on the income distribution because, while education raises wage rates, the extent of the wage differentials across levels of educational attainment will depend on a balancing of demand and supply.

---

17. The measures of schooling are virtually identical in the HIES and the OWS, but it is important to restrict the two surveys to a common age range. Because of the mandatory retirement provisions of the larger enterprises, the OWS excludes a large proportion of older, less-educated workers.

On the demand side, for example, economic advancement is generally associated with an increased demand for more highly skilled workers and an increase in their wages, but an excessively rapid expansion in the supply of skilled workers will generate offsetting pressures, reducing their wages.

The changing distribution of workers by level of educational attainment is shown in Figure 2.8, using data from the HIES. We restricted the sample to male workers between the ages of 25 to 45 to adjust for the previously mentioned difference in the age structure between the HIES and the OWS. On this basis, the two surveys yield very similar results, indicating a remarkable decline in the proportion of the male work force with less than a high school education from 33 percent in 1985 to 2 percent in 2008. Meanwhile, the proportion with a university degree or more has grown from 19 percent in 1985 to 43 percent in 2008.

We can also measure the influence on the change in wage rates across the education categories by estimating a simple regression for each survey year. We use a high school degree as the benchmark and estimate the log of earnings as a function of age, age squared, and categorical variables for the level of education. The time series of the coefficient values

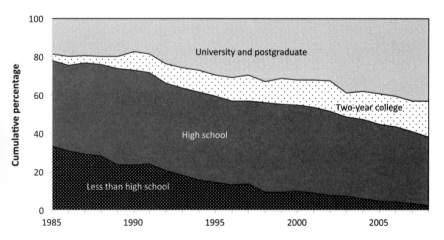

Figure 2.8. Distribution of Male Workers by Educational Attainment in the HIES, Ages 25 to 45, 1985–2008

Distribution shows percentages of all male heads of household who were working and in the age group 25 to 45. *Source:* Computed by the authors from micro-data files of the HIES for the period 1985–2008 (Korea National Statistical Office 2009).

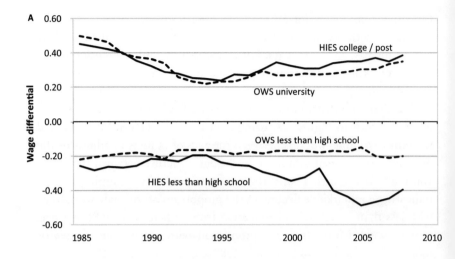

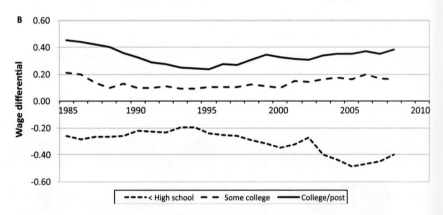

Figure 2.9. Wage Differentials Based on Returns to Education in the HIES and OWS, 1985–2008

(*A*) Earnings differentials, HIES and OWS. (*B*) Earnings differentials, HIES. In both surveys, the comparison is to those with a high school degree. Data are restricted to male heads of household in the HIES and males in the OWS, ages 25 to 45 only. *Source:* Authors' computations, based on the micro-data files of the HIES (Korea National Statistical Office 2009) and OWS (Korean Ministry of Labor 2009).

from the HIES are shown in Figure 2.9. In the mid-1980s college gradu-ates earned a wage premium of about 45 percent compared to those with a high school degree. The premium steadily declined to 24 percent in 1995, but then widened back out to 39 percent in 2008. The pattern is the reverse for those with less than a high school degree, as their wage dis-count also narrowed up until 1994 and widened thereafter. In fact, the widening of the earnings distribution is more pronounced for those with the least education than for those at the top. This general pattern of a widening of the earnings distribution by level of educational attainment is generally consistent with the observed change in the overall earnings distribution.

However, the results for education are not fully reflected in the data of the OWS. While the OWS reveals a very similar change in the pre-mium attached to a college degree, it shows much less deterioration in the relative earnings of those with less than a high school degree. As discussed previously with regard to average wage rates in the HIES and the OWS, we do not fully understand the reasons for these differences. If they were related to firm size, we would expect to observe a change in wage rates within the OWS when the restriction on firm size was lowered from ten to five workers; but that is not evident in the data. The only discrepancy is that the proportion of workers in the OWS with less than a high school education matches that of the HIES in the 1985–1994 period but declines more rapidly in later years. It may be that workers with the least skills are being pushed out of the larger firms that report in the OWS, whereas they are still being captured in the HIES.

Conclusion

Despite the incomplete nature of the survey data, we feel confident in the conclusion that the distribution of income has widened over the past decade both at the family level and in the structure of worker wages. To a large extent this may be due to a changing contribution of educational wage premiums, and we will explore that issue in more detail in a later chapter. Most of the evidence also suggests that the deterioration has been most notable in the lower half of the income distribution, height-ening growing concerns about the prevalence of poverty, the topic of Chapter 3.

CHAPTER 3

The Dimensions of Poverty

Korea has a high level of poverty in comparison with other high-income countries. That is surprising, given its general reputation as having relatively equitable income distribution. Poverty emerged as a serious problem in Korea in the aftermath of the 1997–1998 financial crisis and has remained at an elevated level over the past decade. The problem is very concentrated, however, among the elderly, and rates of poverty are comparatively low for nonelderly households. This is illustrated by a recent OECD report that shows the rate of relative poverty in Korea is among the highest in the OECD, exceeded only by Mexico, Turkey, and the United States (OECD 2008a, 126). Using an income standard of 50 percent of the median, the poverty rate in the middle of the first decade of this century was 15 percent of the population, compared with an OECD average of 11 percent, and 17 percent for the United States. The extent to which poverty is concentrated among the elderly is particularly notable. In the OECD study, Korea had by far the worst poverty rate for those of retirement age—45 percent, compared with an OECD average of only 13 percent.[1] However, poverty is quite low in Korea among households with children. Only 10 percent of children were in households below the poverty threshold, which is below the OECD average of 12 percent and far below the rate in the United States, where 21 percent of children live in households below the poverty level.

---

1. The reported poverty rate was a stunning 69 percent in households with an elderly head who was not working and 77 percent for single-person households (OECD 2008a, 140).

Measurement Issues

Poverty can be defined in two different ways: as an *absolute* standard, based on an inability to meet basic needs, or a *relative* standard that is some percentage (typically, 50 percent) of the median income. Most studies of the evolution of poverty within an individual country emphasize the absolute poverty standard, but international comparisons often use the relative standard because of difficulties in defining basic needs consistently on a cross-national basis. A relative poverty standard is normally of limited interest because it effectively excludes the contribution of economy-wide increases in real incomes as a source of reduced poverty. It is more closely related to the preceding chapter's discussion of income inequality and the distribution of income. However, some international comparisons of poverty extrapolate a relative income measure of a base year on the basis of changes in the price level (OECD 2008a, 130). Such measures should change over time in a pattern closer to that of an absolute poverty standard.

Two methods have been used to establish an absolute standard. The first is to survey actual expenditures of persons who are considered poor, and the second is based on a hypothetical market basket deemed necessary for subsistence. Korea uses the first approach, and the minimum cost of living has been estimated by the Korean government as part of the National Basic Livelihood Security System. It is often used as an informal measure of absolute poverty in the academic studies (see C. Park 2002). Most studies also adjust for household size (equivalized income) and report the poverty rate as a head-count ratio—the share of the population below the poverty threshold.

Detailed estimates of changes in the incidence of poverty within Korea, however, are limited by the previously noted shortage of comprehensive surveys of household income. Until recently, because the Household Income and Expenditure Survey was limited to urban wage-earner households of two or more members, the incomes of many of the most vulnerable members of society, such as the retired and the unemployed, were not reported. In addition, it is difficult to estimate a consistent poverty standard over time. The Korea Institute for Health and Social Affairs (KIHASA) conducted special surveys as part of the effort to establish a minimum cost of living. Those surveys have been used to adjust the income portion of the eligibility standard for the national income support program. In the past, eligibility has also included an asset restriction.

The KIHASA survey results for 1988, 1994, and 1999 are shown in Table 3.1. The three surveys incorporated a common methodology and went beyond the HIES to measure the income of all household types. The table reports the estimated minimum cost of living for families of one to six members. The median income of urban wage-earner households with two or more persons, as reported in the HIES, is included in

Table 3.1. Minimum Monthly Cost of Living, 1988, 1994, and 1999 (thousands of won

Year	Region	Median household income	Household size			
			1-person	*2-person*	*4-person*	*6-persc*
			Minimum monthly cost of living			
1988	Metropolitan		116	191	315	—
	Medium & small cities	543	110	180	297	—
	Rural areas		99	163	268	—
1994	Metropolitan		221	381	714	903
	Medium & small cities	1,481	206	356	666	842
	Rural areas		179	309	579	732
1999	Metropolitan		334	554	958	1,229
	Medium & small cities	1,877	315	521	901	1,156
	Rural areas		271	448	776	995
			Percent of median income			
1988	Medium & small cities	543	20	33	55	—
1994	Medium & small cities	1,481	14	24	45	57
1999	Medium & small cities	1,877	17	28	48	62
			Converted to consumer prices for 2000			
1988	Medium & small cities	1,023	206	340	559	—
1994	Medium & small cities	1,879	262	451	845	1,06
1999	Medium & small cities	1,919	322	533	922	1,18
			Equivalency scales			
1988	Medium & small cities		1.0	1.6	2.7	—
1994	Medium & small cities		1.0	1.7	3.2	4.1
1999	Medium & small cities		1.0	1.7	2.9	3.7

Source: Survey of Korean Institute for Health and Social Affairs, as reported in C. Park (2002), and auth estimates.

Note: Median income is estimated from the HIES for urban households of two or more persons wit wage-earning head.

the first column to provide a benchmark for general income gains over the eleven-year period. The top section of the table shows the estimates of the minimum monthly cost of living for three regional classifications and by family size. The second section reports the minimum cost as a percent of median household income, and the third section adjusts for consumer price changes over the period.

These comparisons highlight the difficulties of constructing a time-consistent poverty standard. The reported minimum cost of living declined relative to median income between 1989 and 1994, but then rose substantially in 1999. The estimate of the minimum cost of living has also increased far more rapidly than the rate of consumer price inflation; the growth between 1988 and 1999 is about twice that implied by an adjustment of the 1999 standard for price changes. In contrast, the bottom section shows a relatively stable estimate of the economies of scale associated with family size across the three surveys.

These surveys and earlier estimates have been used to establish an official poverty line in Korea that is reported in Table 3.2 as a percent of

Table 3.2. Official Poverty Line, 1980–2009 (percent of median household income)

| | Median income (thousands of won per week) | Household size and percent of median income | | | |
		1-person	2-person	4-person	6-person
1980[a]	239	8	17	33	50
1981[a]	239	10	19	38	58
1982	263	9	17	35	52
1983	300	10	21	41	62
1984	331	10	19	39	58
1985	352	10	19	39	58
1986	400	9	19	38	57
1987	468	9	18	37	55
1988	543	8	16	32	49
1989	678	7	14	27	41
1990	805	6	12	24	36
1991	1,000	6	13	26	39

(continued)

Table 3.2. (continued)

	Median income (thousands of won per week)	Household size and percent of median income			
		1-person	2-person	4-person	6-person
1992	1,184	8	17	34	51
1993	1,290	11	22	43	65
1994	1,481	11	23	46	69
1995	1,674	12	24	48	72
1996	1,886	11	22	45	67
1997	2,018	11	22	44	65
1998	1,812	13	25	51	76
1999	1,877	12	25	49	74
2000	2,022	16	27	46	59
2001	2,210	15	25	43	56
2002	2,380	15	24	42	53
2003	2,549	14	23	40	51
2004	2,715	14	22	39	50
2005	2,858	14	23	40	52
2006	3,015	14	23	39	51
2007	3,187	14	23	38	50
2008	3,369	14	23	37	50
2009[a]	3,436	14	24	38	52

Source: C. Park (2002) and authors' estimates.

Note: Values for 1980–1986 are for medium and small cities. Values for the poverty line in other years are national in scope. Prior to 2000, government assistance payments were simply proportionate to family size. More recently, specific measures have been used to determine payments for each household size. Median income is estimated from the HIES for urban households of two or more persons with a wage-earning head.

[a] Values for 1980, 1981, and 2009 are extrapolated by the authors.

the median wage-earner household income for the period from 1980 to 2009 (C. Park 2002). The basic or standard for assistance rose relative to average incomes throughout the 1990s, and since 2000 it has grown in line with the overall growth in median household incomes. The introduction of the National Basic Livelihood Security Act (NBLSA) in 2000 also led to a new specific adjustment for family size in the determination of public assistance payments that was less than the per-person standard of prior years. Thus, it is evident that the official poverty line is a program standard used in the determination of public assistance, and it is not intended to be a time-consistent measure of the level of either absolute or relative poverty incomes. Instead, as overall incomes have grown, the official income assistance programs became relatively more generous. The introduction of the NBLSA in 2000 was particularly important, as it guaranteed households the minimum living standard.

Estimates of the Poverty Rate

Chanyong Park (2002) suggests extending the estimates of the minimal cost of living from the 1994 survey to other years either on the basis of the change in the consumer price index or by the rate of change of consumer expenditures. The adjustment for price change alone implies that the poverty standard will not increase in line with average societal real incomes, and it should yield a rapid decline in the incidence of measured poverty in countries, such as Korea, that have enjoyed large real income gains. On the other hand, the adjustment for growth in average consumption expenditures should yield a measure that roughly parallels the growth in a relative poverty standard. Park extended the 1994 KIHASA survey measure of the minimum standard of living back to 1975 and forward to 2001 using the annual change in household expenditures from the HIES. Using the HIES to measure incomes, he reports a decline in the percent of urban two-person households below his poverty standard, from 22 percent in 1975 to 16 percent by 1990 and a low of 7 percent in 1996.[2] The rate then rises to 19 percent in 1999 at the height of the financial crisis before receding to 10 percent in 2000–2001. While he excludes a significant share of the population, he shows a very rapid rate of progress over the last quarter of the prior century. An updated set of estimates and further discussion are provided in World Bank (2004).

A more recent study is that of Sung (2009). He relied on the estimates of the minimum subsistence income from the Ministry of Health, Welfare, and Family Affairs. Those estimates match the poverty-line measures reported in Table 3.2 for the period since 2000, but the values for the 1990s are considerably higher and closer to the KIHASA estimate of minimum

---

2. Park imputed incomes for nonworker households on the basis of an estimated relationship between consumption and income (C. Park 2002).

living standards. Using data from the HIES, Sung reports an urban poverty rate for disposable income that jumps from a very low 1.5 percent in 1996 to 12.7 percent in 1998, but it then declines quickly to 3.8 percent in 1999 and averages only 2.2 percent over the period from 2001 to 2007. Sung varied the poverty rate for different income measures and reports a very different poverty rate using market incomes (before taxes and excluding transfers) that rises sharply from a low of 2.1 percent in 2001 to 10.9 percent in 2007. The estimates are affected by changes over time in the types of households that are included in the HIES and sharp increases in the official minimum income standard in both 1999 and 2005.

We have constructed alternative measures of the poverty rate that are more consistent and more inclusive of all households than those from the HIES. However, they are available for only a few years. We use the 1996 and 2000 NSHIEs together with the 2006–2008 versions of the HIES, which has been recently expanded to include single-person and rural households.[3] We estimate the absolute poverty rate using the year 2000 size-adjusted minimum income levels established for the National Basic Livelihood Security scheme. That poverty line is extended back to 1996 and forward to 2006 using the changes in the consumer price index. For comparison purposes, we also computed measures of the relative poverty rate. The relative poverty income standard is defined as 50 percent of the median equivalized household income. Equivalized income is computed by dividing household income by the square root of household size.

The estimates of the absolute and relative poverty rates for major socioeconomic groups are reported in Table 3.3. Several aspects stand out. First, although it was increased substantially after the financial crisis, the absolute poverty standard embodied in the welfare program is still very conservative and well below the relative standard of 50 percent of the median. Thus, absolute poverty rates are much lower than those for relative poverty. However, both standards indicate a sharp jump in the pov-

---

3. We worked with a public version of the 2006 HIES survey, which provided data on the income of all households but suppressed information on their employment status beyond distinguishing between households with and without a wage-earner head. That is, unemployed and self-employed household heads are combined because of sampling variability. In addition, we used an annual average of each household's monthly income to improve comparability with the NSHIE; the monthly responses of the HIES have a wider response variation than the annual data of the NSHIE, largely owing to a greater frequency of zero monthly income.

Table 3.3. Absolute and Relative Poverty by Household Type, 1996, 2000, and 2006–2008 (person weights)

	1996	2000	2006–2008
Absolute poverty			
All households	3.8	6.9	6.5
No elderly member	2.5	4.8	4.0
Elderly member	8.6	13.4	14.0
Elderly household head	13.5	16.1	17.0
Elderly household head alone	39.1	45.7	26.3
Household head with aged dependent	3.3	6.5	6.5
Nonelderly, no children	1.8	3.4	5.0
Nonelderly, with children	2.8	5.5	4.1
Relative poverty[a]			
All households	8.4	11.5	12.9
No elderly member	6.1	8.5	8.2
Elderly member	17.1	20.9	27.5
Elderly household head	25.9	25.6	31.4
Elderly household head alone	71.6	74.7	65.8
Household head with aged dependent	7.6	9.4	11.1
Nonelderly, no children	6.4	7.7	10.4
Nonelderly, with children	6.3	8.9	8.0

Source: Korea National Statistical Office (2002) for 1996, 2000; Korea National Statistical Office (2009) for 2006–2008.

Note: Elderly is defined as 60 years of age and older.

[a] Relative poverty is defined as income below 50% of the median household equivalized income (income/sqrt[size]) using person weights.

erty rate between 1996 and 2000 that can be attributed to the financial crisis, and the poverty rate has remained at elevated levels after 2000. The overall rate of absolute poverty jumps from 3.8 percent in 1996 to 6.9 percent in 2000, and decreases slightly to an average of 6.5 percent in 2006–2008. The corresponding relative rates are 8.4, 11.5, and 12.9 percent.[4] Second, as reported for the OECD comparisons of relative poverty, there

---

4. Our poverty rates for 2006 are markedly higher than those of Sung. Part of the explanation is that our indexed poverty standard is about 8 percent below the official measure in 2006, but we have not been able to fully reconcile the two estimates.

is an extraordinarily high incidence of poverty among Koreans age 60 and up who are living in independent households. At 17 percent for aged couples and 26 percent for the elderly living alone in 2006–2008, the absolute poverty rate for aged persons living in their own household is four to six times that of persons in households without an aged member. Third, the incidence of poverty among the nonaged has been consistently low, although it did jump sharply at the time of the financial crisis. Finally, Korea does particularly well in limiting poverty within households with children.

The high rate of poverty among the elderly can be traced to the still immature state of the national pension system; with a limited number of years of contribution, older workers qualify for only a minimal pension or none at all.[5] They need to continue working to have a source of income. But under current practices, older workers face a high risk of job loss. Retention rates fall sharply in many large firms, which often impose mandatory retirement at about age 55, and even though workers are likely to find a new job relatively quickly, the replacement jobs are often of low quality and low pay. Currently, Korea has no legislation on age discrimination, and firms prefer an early mandatory retirement age in a pay system that emphasizes large seniority wage premiums. Many new jobs are advertised with age restrictions.

In addition, the Korean labor market has become increasingly bifurcated. Regular workers at large unionized firms receive a full range of social benefits and have considerable employment security. In contrast, nonregular workers often work with temporary contracts and are responsible for making their own contributions to the public pension and health care systems.[6] Temporary employment has grown from 17 percent of all employment in 2001 to 29 percent in 2006 (Grubb, Lee, and Tergeist 2007). The problem grew more severe in the 2008–2009 financial crisis, as layoffs were concentrated among the nonregular work force. The 2007 Irregular Worker Law called for the conversion of irregular workers to regular status after two years, but with the financial crisis, many firms chose to terminate those workers rather than bear the costs and face the strictures of regular employment. Unfortunately, the income and wage surveys do not include a consistent definition of nonregular employment

5. The pension system is discussed more fully in Chapter 6.
6. See J. Ahn (2004) for a more thorough discussion.

that could be used to judge its role in the widening of incomes and in the creation of poverty.

International Comparisons

Cross-national comparisons of the poverty rates and the income distribution are difficult because of substantial difference in the scope of the various national surveys. As we have found with the Korean surveys, important subpopulations are often excluded. The OECD has devoted considerable resources to the identification of differences in scope and income concepts and worked to produce a set of standardized measures for member countries. The most recent conclusions are available in a 2008 collection of tables on various measures of income distribution and poverty rates (OECD 2008a). For the 30 high-income countries included in the analysis, the OECD reports a moderate but pervasive trend toward increased income inequality over the past two decades. In addition, overall poverty rates—as noted earlier—have generally risen, with declines in the poverty of the elderly being offset by increases among families with children.

In the comparison, Korea is close to the OECD average in terms of summary measures of inequality, such as the Gini coefficient, or interdecile ratios applied to household disposable income. However, it is an outlier with respect to the very small magnitude of redistribution that is achieved through government tax and transfer policies. Korea has the smallest share of both public transfers and direct taxes in household incomes. Thus, to a greater extent than in the other countries, its income distribution is a reflection of market incomes, not government tax and transfer policies. As noted above, Korea does less well in the poverty rankings, where its overall poverty rate is near the top of the distribution, together with Japan and the United States. Using data from establishment surveys, Korea reported levels of overall wage inequality in 2006 that were exceeded only by the United States, and for the 50/10 decile ratio—the bottom half of the wage distribution— Korea reported the largest value (OECD 2008b). It also has the largest gender wage gap.[7]

---

7. The wage gap is defined as the difference between median earnings of men and women as a percentage of the male median.

Table 3.4. Comparisons of Inequality and Relative Poverty: Korea, Taiwan, and the United States, 1996, 2000, and 2006

	1996	2000	2006
Korea[a]			
Gini coefficient	0.326	0.393	0.375
90/10 ratio	4.90	7.05	8.05
90/50 ratio	1.94	2.15	2.17
50/10 ratio	2.52	3.27	3.72
Relative poverty			
All households	8.4	11.5	12.6
With elderly member	17.1	20.9	27.2
Nonelderly, with children	6.3	8.9	7.8
Taiwan[b]			
Gini coefficient	0.313	0.326	0.345
90/10 Ratio	4.63	5.11	5.62
90/50 Ratio	1.97	2.03	2.12
50/10 Ratio	2.35	2.52	2.65
Relative poverty			
All households	4.8	5.0	6.0
With elderly member	7.8	8.4	10.4
Nonelderly, with children	3.0	3.1	3.0
United States			
Gini coefficient	0.454	0.460	0.468
90/10 Ratio	10.38	10.65	11.27
90/50 Ratio	2.63	2.68	2.76
50/10 Ratio	3.95	3.98	4.09
Relative poverty			
All households	21.2	20.5	21.1
With elderly member	15.0	15.5	19.3
Nonelderly, with children	21.9	20.9	21.8

Source: Korea National Statistical Office (2002 and 2009); Republic of China (2007); and United States Census Bureau (2009).

[a] IES 2006 values for Korea are annual averages of monthly observations.

[b] 2006 values are 2005 for Taiwan.

Note: Elderly is defined as 60 years of age and older; children are defined as those 19 years of age and younger.

Table 3.4 provides an alternative comparison of the patterns of change in the income distribution and poverty rates in Korea, Taiwan, and the United States over the past decade.[8] Taiwan is introduced as a comparator country within Asia because of the similarity of its growth experience over the past half century and the fact that its current level of income per capita is only slightly above that of Korea. Both countries have attracted considerable international attention because of the rapid pace of their economic development. We also had access to the micro-data file of a household survey for Taiwan that is similar to those for Korea and the United States.

Income distribution in Korea is slightly more unequal than in Taiwan. The differences are concentrated in the bottom portions of the distribution, as shown by the higher values of the 50/10 decile ratio in Korea. Both countries have experienced a widening of the distribution over the past decade. The contrasts are most striking, however, with respect to the poverty measures. Korea has a much higher overall incidence of *relative* poverty, and the differences are very dramatic for the elderly (something we expected from the OECD comparison), but Korea also has a higher rate of poverty among households with children. Poverty rates have drifted up in both countries over the past decade.

Inequality is not as pronounced in Korea, however, as it is within the United States. Both the Gini and the interdecile ratios suggest a more equal income distribution. However, Korea and Taiwan have had more rapid rates of deterioration than in the United States. Likewise, overall rates of relative poverty are lower than in the United States, although the incidence of poverty among the elderly is higher in Korea.

Conclusion

Poverty in Korea is unusually concentrated among the aged. It is very low among the young and those of working age, but it is extremely high among the older, retired generations. The low rate of poverty among the young reflects the relatively narrow range of wage rates in the bottom half of the wage distribution and the low overall rates of unemployment. However, the rate of poverty among the elderly is much higher in Korea

---

8. The estimates for Korea in 2006 are annual averages of each household's monthly income, taken from the expanded HIES. The use of the monthly averages improves comparability both with previous years taken from the NSHIE and with the structure of the comparator-country surveys.

than in other countries at comparable stages of development. This reflects several factors. First, the extraordinary speed of economic development meant that the savings accumulated during the years of low wages contributed relatively little to the cost of retirement in the advanced modern economy of today. Second, Korea was slow to establish a public retirement system, and when it did, it opted for a funded system in which benefits are dependent on a long history of contributions to the system. Hence, the currently retired receive very small benefit amounts and they will continue to do so for another decade. And third, while Korea has the structure of a modern social insurance system, the payments are limited and constitute a small share of household income.

PART II

Socioeconomic Determinants of
Inequality and Poverty

The evident worsening of the income distribution in Korea after the 1997–1998 crisis has been a source of major public discontent and has generated a large number of studies aimed at identifying its causes. A widening of the income range is a shared phenomenon in many advanced economies in which the various national studies have found some common features. To begin with, we can identify several direct factors— including education (skill), family size, and the age and number of workers in the family—that have obvious effects on the level of family income. In the case of Korea, these determinants may be changing in ways that differ from the pre-crisis era when the income distribution was becoming more equal. In addition, the institutional and economic environments in Korea have changed dramatically since the pre-crisis era; democratization, market opening, capital market liberalization, and alterations in the labor market may have exercised significant indirect effects on the distribution of income and wealth.

In this portion of our study we examine in greater detail the potential role within Korea of changes in these institutional and socioeconomic factors. Some argue that these developments require that Korea design a new model to promote future growth with equity, and that the old policy emphasis on maximizing growth with only a secondary focus on equity cannot be maintained. Because of the prominent role that Korea has played as a counterexample to Simon Kuznets's 1955 hypothesis of a negative association between growth and equity, we begin in Chapter 4 with an analysis of the relationship between economic growth and the income distribution. Kuznets argued that as labor shifts from sectors with low productivity to sectors with high productivity, aggregate inequality will increase initially and decrease only at later stages of development. (In an alternative argument, Kaldor [1978] postulated an inverse relationship because the concentration of income in the hands of the rich, who have a high marginal propensity to save, would promote a high level of saving and rapid growth.) The interaction between economic growth and income inequality is a highly contentious issue in the literature on economic development, in part because of the frequent allegation that growth yields insufficient benefits for the poor. We address this issue from the traditional perspective of the relationship between growth and the *level* of income inequality, and from a more dynamic perspective in which poverty rates and the *change* in income at different positions in the distribution are linked to growth in both aggregate GDP and average household income.

In Chapter 5, we examine some of the major factors that have been the focus of studies of income inequality in other countries. First, we look at the influence of demographic change. This is important at the aggregate level because of the extraordinarily sharp decline in the Korean fertility rate over the past several decades and the resulting rapid aging of the population; however, there is also potential for change at the family level, owing to the rise in the number of multiple-earner families and a trend toward smaller family units. Second, we consider how the impressive speed with which Korea was able to raise the educational attainment of its work force has contributed to changes in income distribution. Concerns about trends in educational improvements have been central to the discussion of changes in the income distribution of countries such as the United States, and the pattern of improvements may have changed recently in Korea. Third, we investigate the role of trade openness or globalization in a broader context. Trade openness is usually understood to mean the ease with which goods and services move across national borders in response to reductions in tariffs and other barriers. It is often captured internationally by the ratio of trade to GDP, and serves as one of the most contentious explanatory factors, as is evident from the increasing public outcries against "globalization." Finally, we briefly focus on the labor market and, in particular, the influence of the growing reliance on irregular workers, who differ in their contractual relationships with employers. Since the labor market in Korea is more rigid than in many industrial countries, this issue has received attention as firms look for ways to become more flexible and competitive in serving international markets.

CHAPTER 4

Effects of Growth on Inequality and Poverty

Korea has sustained a high economic growth rate for the past 30 years—averaging 10 percent annually—for which it has attracted extensive international attention. Such rapid progress was achieved largely through the government's export-oriented economic policy, which considered growth a matter of the highest priority. The equality of distribution within the process of high growth was relatively neglected as a policy goal, owing to the principle of growth first and distribution later—the idea that if growth is achieved, distribution issues will be solved naturally. And indeed, after the mid-1980s the distribution structure did show steady improvement.

The currency crisis in 1997–1998 is viewed as a turning point for the discussion of distribution issues in Korea.[1] Poverty and unemployment rates increased, greatly altering the structure of the income distribution and raising measures of inequality nearly back to the levels of the late 1970s. More worrisome, the increase in inequality proved not to be temporary, and the new higher levels of inequality persisted over the past decade.

The Korean economy originally achieved its high growth on the basis of a labor-intensive industrial structure combined with relatively cheap labor. As international competition has intensified and incomes have risen, that growth strategy has lost its relevance. In the twenty-first century,

---

1. We argued in Chapter 2 that the prior narrowing of the income distribution is actually apparent in the data for several years prior to the crisis. Nevertheless, the magnitudes of the spikes in the measures of income inequality at the time of the crisis clearly mark it as the psychological inflection point of the debate.

the country will require a strong capital base and improvements in the level of technology if it is to remain competitive. In the transition to an industrial structure based on capital and technology, however, job opportunities and income will increase for workers who are well educated and highly skilled and decrease for those who are not. Thus the change in the growth pattern of the Korean economy is likely to gradually widen the distribution structure. In addition, it is highly possible that other changes in the environment of the Korean economy, such as increased market opening and population aging, may also lead to a worsening of income equality within the population. Though the argument that market-opening policies generally raise a country's average level of income is widely accepted, the gains in income may go predominately to the higher-income classes.[2] Additionally, because the rapid aging of the population in Korea implies an increase in the elderly population, which has typically had a relatively low level of income, the aging process could also have a deleterious effect on the distribution of incomes.

As the nation prepares new policies to deal with the changed circumstances of the twenty-first century, research on how growth and distributional issues interact within these changing socioeconomic circumstances takes on great importance. The first step toward understanding this interaction is to review past research examining the relationship between growth and the income distribution from both a theoretical and an empirical perspective, and apply it to Korea's situation.

Economic Growth and the Distribution of the Gains

In his work on economic growth and income inequality, Simon Kuznets (1955) hypothesized that in the early stages of economic development the distribution of income will initially worsen as average incomes increase, but will tend to improve in later stages with higher levels of income per capita. This inverted-U hypothesis, with its implication that growth might be bad for the poor, has been the subject of numerous international

---

2. The World Bank and others have released research results that show that market opening does not influence the distribution of income within a country. However, according to Lee and Park (2002), those studies reached a wrong conclusion because of their methodological problems. We will discuss this point further in later sections of this chapter.

studies.[3] After an initial period of support, the hypothesis has come under increasing attack in recent decades both because of the expansion of the analysis to a larger and more diverse set of developing countries and because several high-income countries—the United States in particular—have shown a reversal in the equalizing trend.

In their initial development, Korea and other East Asian countries were frequently cited as exceptions to Kuznets's hypothesis. Birdsall, Ross, and Sabot (1995) argued that the hypothesis did not apply to those countries because of the emphasis they placed on education to expand the supply of highly skilled workers, and an export-oriented growth policy to increase the demand for relatively unskilled workers, as well as their significant investments in the agricultural sector; it may be that the structure of the growth policies in Korea and other East Asian countries altered what would otherwise have been a negative correlation between growth and the equality of the income distribution.

The Korean economy has maintained a high growth rate since the 1960s, when economic growth began in earnest, but there is a limited amount of data on the distribution of income in the early decades of growth, and there are relatively few formal studies.[4] During the early years of economic expansion, the condition of the income distribution was not a primary focus of Korean researchers, and when inequality showed signs of improvement during the 1980s, interest in distributional issues fell further. After the currency crisis in 1997, however, the income distribution worsened markedly and became a major social issue, and then the volume of research expanded rapidly.[5] Still, those studies focused on the relatively brief period of the late 1990s, so they are not suitable for evaluating the long-term changes in the income distribution within Korea.

The study that examined the income distribution over the longest time period was conducted by Yoon (1997), who measured the Gini coefficient of household income from 1963 to 1993 using the Urban Household Survey. We use the estimates of the Gini coefficients from Yoon's research

---

3. The international evidence on Kuznets's hypothesis is examined by Adelman and Morris (1973) and Ahluwalia (1976a, 1976b).

4. Examples of some early work are studies by Choo (1982) and Choo and Yoon (1984).

5. Jung (2000), W. Lee (2000), Kim and Topel (1995), K.-S. Choi (1996), G. Yoo (1998), and S. Park (2000).

and extend his measures of the Gini coefficients of household income from 1993 to 2008 with the data shown previously in Figure 2.6. Our results are presented in Figure 4.1, which shows the trend of the Gini coefficient from 1963 to 2008. The income distribution of Korea showed signs of improvement in the 1960s, worsened in the 1970s, improved again from the late 1970s to the early 1990s, and has deteriorated since.

A study by An (2003) analyzed the relationship between the income distribution and growth in Korea using the logarithm of national income per capita and the Gini coefficient from 1963 to 2000. Using various empirical methods, he concluded that Kuznets's inverted-U hypothesis was not supported in Korea—changes in income levels had no consistent influence on the distribution of income. Factors such as the level of human capital, market opening, and population aging, however, were found to have large influences.

An also divided the relationship between growth and inequality in Korea into four periods. In the first, from 1963 to 1971, income inequality was reduced. This is perhaps because the preceding postwar years had been a time of political instability in which the class of the urban poor increased greatly, while economic development after 1962 began to create new jobs that lead to a decline in the numbers of urban poor.

The second period extended from 1971 to the late 1970s, another period of political instability, this time due to the global oil crisis and the controversies in Korea surrounding the Park administration's Constitution for Revitalizing Reform. During this time the income distribution

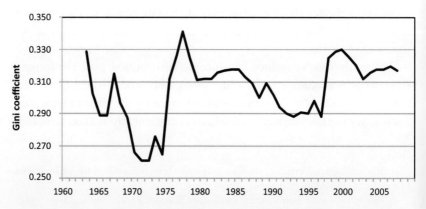

Figure 4.1. Trend of Income Distribution, Gini Coefficient, 1963–2008
Source: Yoon (1997), Korea National Statistical Office (2009), and authors' calculations.

widened, as income levels increased substantially for the top percentiles. The benefits of strong economic growth were concentrated among a select few, and income inequality increased.

The third period, from the late 1970s to the early 1990s, saw a gradual reduction of income inequality. The Korean economy reached almost full employment in this period, and the wages of salaried workers rose sharply. Furthermore, through the democratization process, social and economic benefits were extended to include classes of Koreans who had been neglected in the past (Yoon 1997).

The equalizing pattern ended around 1993, when the measures of income inequality again began to rise. While there was a large spike in inequality after the currency crisis of 1997, the reversal actually started prior to the crisis. It has been attributed to a wide range of economic factors, such as market openness and the introduction of an annual salary system with performance-based pay, as well as to noneconomic factors like the increase in the divorce rate and the rise in the number of elderly citizens, thanks to population aging (Sung 2001).

Factors Other than Growth That Influence Income Inequality

When looking into the relationship between growth and the distribution of income, understanding the role of a country's special political, economic, and social conditions is more important than testing Kuznets's hypothesis. In the case of Korea, it is necessary to train a special focus on the worsening of the income distribution after the early 1990s. Although the inequality has shown some signs of lessening in recent years, that improvement should be viewed as a correction to the spike in inequality during the currency crisis, not as a new trend. Korea is still experiencing a long-term worsening of the income distribution that extends back to the early 1990s.

The World Bank (2002) asserts that the increase in economic freedom resulting from greater market openness produces more economic wealth, and that it does not have a consistent effect on the income distribution of individual countries. Lee and Park (2002), however, argue that the World Bank analysis is static, as it looked at countries whose markets were already very open prior to the review period in 2000. They instead conduct a dynamic analysis using data over the period of 1997 to 2000. According to their findings, an increase in openness resulted in greater inequality in 2000 compared with 1997, with a larger effect for countries that had high levels of economic freedom. They therefore conclude the opposite of the World Bank—that increases in economic freedom due to market opening do increase inequality. The study by An (2003) also supports Lee and Park's findings in the specific case of Korea; he showed that as the ratio of the foreign direct investment rate to GDP and the ratio of private capital flows to GDP increase, the Gini coefficient also increases.

Although market opening may have highly favorable effects on overall incomes, it is likely to induce a rise in inequality in an economy with Korea's skill mix. A more open market structure allows the well educated an opportunity to increase their incomes in a larger market where their skills are relatively scarce. In contrast, the less educated face greater competition in a global economy where their skill characteristics are more plentiful than in the domestic market; hence inequality is likely to increase.

We should not hold a negative view of market opening simply because it might increase income inequality, since market opening offers an important opportunity for a still-developing country like Korea to approach the average incomes of the advanced economies. The rate of economic growth increased much more for developing countries than for advanced countries after market opening, and the inequality between countries declined (Lee and Park 2002). The most important challenge for Koreans in the twenty-first century will be to grasp the array of growth opportunities from market opening while working to offset the worsening of inequality that it may induce domestically.

Population aging is a general phenomenon that results from economic progress, social stability, and the development of medical technology. Factors like urbanization linked to economic progress, an increase in nuclear families, a decrease in the birth rate owing to an increase in women's economic activities, and a drop in the death rate due to the development of medical technology have contributed to the increase in the proportion of the elderly in most countries. In the case of the major advanced countries, the proportion of the elderly (those over the age of 65) has already reached 20 percent. Their proportion in Korea passed 7 percent in 2000, indicating its entrance as an aging society.[6]

---

6. The UN categorizes countries according to the age structure of their population. Countries with an elderly population (age 65 and up) that makes up less than 4 percent of the total population are characterized as young-population countries, if the proportion

An (2003) showed that as the proportion of the population that is aged increases, the Gini coefficient tends to rise as well. This is because the average income of elderly households in Korea is far less than the average income of nonelderly households. According to An, Kim, and Jeon (2002), the poverty rate among elderly Korean households is more than twice that of nonelderly households, and even larger differences have been found, as discussed in Chapter 3. A sharp increase in the elderly population is likely to lead to an increase in the number of households in poverty and a worsening of the income distribution.

Sung and Park (2009) studied population aging and its distributional effects using the 1998 through 2008 HIES data sets, and predicted its future effects on income inequality up to 2050. They found that the changes in income inequality were mostly induced by economic factors (that is, business cycles) between 1982 and 1994. They argued, however, that while those changes in income inequality were dominated by economic factors, population aging began to significantly affect income inequality starting in the mid-1990s, and its effect has continued to grow with time. From 2005 onward, the marginal contributions of economic factors to the changes in income inequality have almost disappeared, and the changes in income inequality are now driven almost solely by the population's aging. Sung and Park also forecast the future values of income inequality, incorporating the increasing effects of population aging on income inequality. In their 2009 study, which uses the population forecasts of Statistics Korea, income inequality, measured in terms of the squared coefficient of variation, is expected to be 27.5 percent greater in 2050 than in 2008, solely because of population aging.

Because, as their findings suggest, income inequality will worsen in the future due to the rapid aging of the population, economic policies aimed at mitigating inequality will not be sufficient. They will need to be combined with policies to strengthen the welfare programs directed toward the elderly, if they are to address the whole problem. In addition, to minimize the socioeconomic impact of aging more research should be conducted on its consequences and potential solutions. In situations like Korea's, where the aging of the population is proceeding very rapidly, such research becomes more urgent. Preparing for an aging population,

---

is 4 to 7 percent the country is classified as a mature population, and countries where more than 7 percent of the population is elderly are aged-population countries.

which has taken decades in other countries, has to be undertaken in just a few years in Korea.

Population aging is also an increasingly important element of the nation's poverty problem. Sung (2010) argues that prior to the first decade of this century, most adult members of poor households were unemployed or working-poor. The composition of poor households is changing quickly, however, and the majority of households in the lowest income decile now consist of retirees. The acceleration of population aging likely will lead to a similar phenomenon in the near future for the second lowest decile. Sung asserts that the poverty problem caused by population aging is different from the one caused by economic factors, such as changes in unemployment rates or business cycles, so focusing on job creation may not be enough to solve it.

Sung (2010) also raises the issue of the relationship between the physical and the economic length of life. In the past, the pace of technical development was sufficiently slow that skills workers accumulated when they were young were sufficient to serve them throughout their work life. Therefore, the concerns about future job security were mostly confined to questions about the physical condition of older workers. The rapid evolution of technology has led to a potential shortening of the worker's economic life cycle, such that older workers who no longer have the necessary technical skills to stay competitive are replaced by younger workers before they are ready for retirement. Thus, rapid development of technology and the ensuing industrial restructuring lead to a shortening of the economic life cycle of a worker. This creates an imbalance between the economic and physical life cycles that magnifies the poverty problem, as older workers are forced out of jobs and join the ranks of the impoverished retirees—where they remain for a longer time, due to the increase in longevity.

Dynamic Effects on Inequality and Poverty

Economic crisis and stagnation result in unemployment, which worsens both poverty and inequality. This suggests that the relationship between economic growth and income inequality may differ over the business cycle. Previous studies, however, have not considered the influence of business cycle fluctuations and have merely focused on finding a uniform

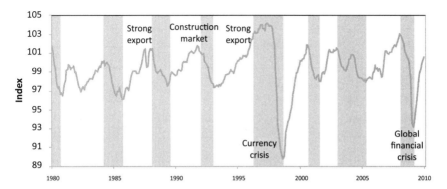

Figure 4.2. The Business Cycle in Korea, 1980–2010
Graph shows cyclical coincident index; ratio to five-year centered average. Shaded areas indicate business recessions. *Source:* Korea National Statistical Office (2006a) and authors' calculations.

relationship between growth and inequality. They also have not addressed the effects of variation in rates of economic growth. In other words, most researchers construct their analysis to connect the level of national per capita income or gross domestic product with the extent of inequality in each period. Yet, as shown in Figure 4.2, the Korean economy has been subject to large periodic swings in business activity. The figure displays the composite coincident business-cycle indicator compiled by Statistics Korea and the timing of the various business cycles, dating back to 1980. There are several episodes of business-cycle downturn, of which the currency crisis of 1997–1998 and the global financial crisis of 2008–2009 are the most severe.

We can conduct a more detailed examination of changes in the income distribution by looking at the distribution of income across individual classes. In Table 4.1, we summarize the shares of household income for five classes: the bottom three income deciles, the fourth through the sixth, the seventh through the ninth, and the top decile. Between 1985 and the mid-1990s, the income shares of the lower- and middle-income classes were rising at the expense of the share accruing to the top decile. The share of the lowest three deciles peaked in 1993, fell sharply during the crisis, and continued to deteriorate even after recovery from the crisis, reaching a minimum of 12.8 percent in 2005. In contrast, the share accruing to the middle- and upper-middle income

Table 4.1. Shares of Household Income in Korea, by Income Decile, 1979–2005

	1st–3rd deciles	4th–6th deciles	7th–9th deciles	10th decile	Ratio (10th/1st decile)
1979	14.0	24.4	38.2	23.5	7.6
1980	14.0	24.6	38.0	23.4	7.6
1981	14.3	24.6	38.0	23.0	7.3
1982	14.0	24.3	37.8	24.0	8.2
1983	14.1	24.0	37.9	24.0	7.7
1984	13.8	24.2	38.0	24.0	8.0
1985	14.0	24.1	37.6	24.3	8.3
1986	14.0	24.2	38.0	23.8	8.1
1987	14.0	24.3	38.2	23.4	8.0
1988	14.4	24.3	37.9	23.5	7.5
1989	14.5	24.2	37.7	23.7	7.5
1990	14.8	24.6	37.9	22.8	7.1
1991	15.1	25.0	38.0	21.9	6.6
1992	15.1	25.4	38.2	21.3	6.5
1993	15.2	25.2	38.1	21.6	6.5
1994	15.1	25.3	38.4	21.3	6.3
1995	14.9	25.2	38.4	21.5	6.5
1996	14.5	25.1	39.0	21.4	6.8
1997	14.7	25.4	39.0	20.9	6.7
1998	13.6	25.1	39.4	21.9	8.3
1999	13.5	24.9	39.5	22.2	8.2
2000	13.6	25.0	39.1	22.3	7.9
2001	13.5	24.5	39.3	22.6	7.8
2002	13.7	24.7	39.1	22.6	7.6
2003	13.4	25.1	39.0	22.6	9.0
2004	12.8	25.0	39.3	22.8	9.7
2005	12.8	25.2	39.5	22.4	9.2

Source: Korea National Statistical Office (2009) and authors' estimates.
Note: Business cycles, shown by shaded areas, are defined by Korea National Statistical Office (2006b).

groups (deciles 4–9) remained quite stable. The biggest change was for the top decile, whose share fell substantially in the decade prior to the crisis, but reversed that trend and rose substantially in the crisis and post-crisis years. The top decile's share in 2004, 9.7 percent, was the highest in a quarter century. The ratio of the share of income accruing to the tenth versus the first decile fell from 8.3 in 1985 to a low of 6.3 in 1994, before rising to a peak of 9.7 in 2004.

While there are some exceptions, the lowest income deciles tend to have an increase in their share during expansionary periods and a decline during periods of contraction, which implies that they are more sensitive to business fluctuations than other income classes.

To analyze how fluctuations in economic activity affect the real wages of each income class, we employ a simple estimation model using annual data from the HIES for 1979 to 2005. We compute real wage income for each income class and real GDP (excluding production in agriculture, forestry, and fisheries). We estimate the following logarithmic relationship:

$$\Delta \ln y_i = \beta_0 \Delta \ln GDP_i + \beta_1 \Delta \ln GDP_i * BC + \beta_2 \Delta \ln y_{i-1} + \beta_3 \ln y_{i-1} + \beta_4 \Delta \ln GDP_{i-1} + \varepsilon_i$$

where,

y_i = real income per income class,
GDP = nonagricultural gross domestic product, and
BC = a categorical variable for the stage of the business cycle (expansion = 1 and downturn = 0)

The results of this analysis are reported in Table 4.2. They are limited to every other decile without loss of any significance.

Our first finding is that the estimated coefficient measuring the short-term effect of GDP growth (the first difference of log nonfarm GDP [ΔGDP]) on income is significant for all income classes and ranges from 0.848 ~ 1.682, with larger coefficients associated with the lower income levels. The coefficient for the first decile is the largest, which indicates that the short-term effect of variations in economic activity is greatest for the lowest income class. The estimated regression coefficient for the first decile of 1.682 means that when the nonfarming GDP increases by 1 percent, the income of the first decile increases by 1.682 percent.

Table 4.2. Results of Regression Analysis by Income Decile, Selected Deciles, 1979–2005

	1st decile	3rd decile	5th decile	7th decile	9th decile	10th decile
ΔGDP	1.68***	1.12***	1.08***	0.99***	0.98***	0.85***
	(7.4)	(5.6)	(7.4)	(7.0)	(7.4)	(6.6)
ΔGDP×BC	0.57**	0.24*	0.16	0.15	0.13	0.04
	(2.4)	(1.8)	(1.4)	(1.3)	(0.9)	(0.3)
Δy(−1)	0.08	0.31***	0.30***	0.28***	0.20***	0.16
	(0.9)	(5.6)	(4.4)	(5.5)	(2.6)	(1.6)
y(−1)	−0.14	−0.12***	−0.12***	−0.10***	−0.08***	−0.04*
	(1.5)	(2.7)	(3.4)	(3.7)	(3.0)	(1.8)
ΔGDP(−1)	0.14	0.13***	0.13***	0.11***	0.09***	0.05*
	(1.4)	(2.7)	(3.4)	(3.7)	(3.0)	(1.8)
R^2	0.77	0.78	0.82	0.84	0.76	0.60
D.W.	1.8	2.3	2.3	2.3	2.6	2.6

Source: Authors' calculations, based on HIES data for 1979–2005 (Korea National Statistical Office 2009).
Note: ***, **, and * indicate statistical significance at the 1-percent, 5-percent, and 10-percent levels, respectively; t-values are in parentheses.

Our second finding illuminates how the effect of economic growth on incomes at different portions of the distribution varies according to the stage of the business cycle. Using an interaction variable of Δ*GDP* multiplied by the stage of the business fluctuation variable (*BC*), we find that the regression coefficients of the first and third deciles are 0.569 and 0.236, respectively, and are statistically significant. This means that during the business expansion, the income elasticity of the first and third deciles increases more than other income classes. The income elasticity of the first decile is especially large at 0.569, which can be interpreted as a pro-cyclical effect. In summary, all income classes in Korea are influenced by variations in economic growth, but the effect appears to be larger and asymmetric for the low-income classes.

Income Mobility

Our prior analysis supports the Korean public's perception that income inequality has worsened since the financial crisis—that as the rich get richer, the poor become poorer. However, the problems of inequality would be mitigated if this were a transitory phenomenon in a society in

Table 4.3. Annual Transition Probabilities, Disposable Income, Two-Year
Averages 1998–2007 (percent)

	1999–2001	2001–2003	2003–2005	2005–2007
Remaining in the same decile	28.2	29.8	33.3	36.7
Moving one decile up	17.0	16.1	18.1	18.1
Moving two deciles up	8.3	8.2	7.6	7.1
Moving one decile down	15.5	17.7	17.9	16.4
Moving two deciles down	9.2	8.3	7.6	7.1
More than two deciles up	10.9	10.1	7.9	7.7
More than two deciles down	11.0	9.9	7.8	7.0

Source: Authors' calculations based on data from the Korean Labor and Income Panel Study (Korea Labor Institute 2007).
Note: The annual transitions are reported as two-year averages.

which it was relatively easy to move up the socioeconomic ladder. Thus, estimating the degree of income mobility—the ease with which people can transition from lower to higher economic status—can complement the standard measures of inequality by adding a dynamic aspect to an otherwise static observation.

Generally, income mobility is measured by the extent of movement of individuals (or households) across income classes over time. Measurement of income mobility therefore requires a survey with a panel dimension, in which respondents are followed over several years. We use data from the Korean Labor and Income Panel Study (KLIPS) for 1999 to 2007 and focus on trends in relative income mobility, which is measured by the change of the rank within the income distribution.[7] Also, we try to analyze how the mobility differs by the demographic characteristic of household head.

We adopt the concept of the transition matrix used by Shorrocks (1978) to compute relative income mobility. The transition matrix reveals

7. The survey follows a representative sample of households over time, with follow-up interviews being conducted on an annual basis.

who is moving from one income class to another class in the distribution. In this context, each cell of the transition matrix is the probability p_{ij} of transferring from decile i to decile j in period t to t+1. Those indicators are summarized in Table 4.3 for the eight waves of the KLIPS between 1999 and 2007.

Our calculations suggest that Korea is a relatively mobile society, but that income mobility has decreased over the 1999–2007 period.[8] As shown in the first row of Table 4.3, the proportion of households that remained in the same decile of the income distribution from one year to the next increased from 28.2 percent in 1999–2001 to 36.7 percent in 2005–2007. The decline in mobility is particularly evident in the reduced probability of moving two or more deciles and suggests a further dimension in which income inequality has worsened.

We also computed the transitional probabilities for male- and female-headed households and by the age of the household head. We found that households with a male head were more likely to change their position in the income distribution than those with a female head, suggesting a lower degree of income mobility for female-headed households. Mobility rates across age groups are very uniform, except for a marked decline in mobility for households whose head is age 70 and older.

Sung (2011) proposes an alternative measure of income mobility based on the assumption that household income has a log-normal distribution. He used the KLIPS data for the period from 1998 to 2008 and found that income mobility had declined by a statistically significant amount in recent years, confirming our findings with Shorrocks's measure. The downward trend in income mobility suggests that the observed increase in income inequality is not simply the result of random short-run factors, and that Korea requires an expansion of welfare policies to cope with long-term or even lifelong poverty.

---

8. Comparable calculations for the United States are available in Bradbury and Katz (2009).

CHAPTER 5

The Influence of Population Aging, Education, and Globalization

Increased concern about income inequality in many countries has given rise to a vast amount of research to determine the main causes. Three causes that have been identified are of particular relevance to Korea. First, the country is in the midst of large-scale demographic change, as an unusually sharp decline in the birth rate and an increase in life expectancy have combined to produce a rapidly aging population. This strikes us as very pertinent because of the high rate of poverty we found for the aged in Korea (see Chapter 3) and because of arguments that Korea has an unusually rigid wage structure that places a high emphasis on seniority. Second, we know from the analysis in Chapter 2 that education has been a major determinant of earnings in Korea, and it is possible that changes in the balance of the supply and demand for workers of different skill levels have altered the wage structure. Third, the increased globalization of the economy has expanded competition with workers in other countries, and a global labor market may embody a much different mix of labor skills than that found in the domestic economy. Finally, we include a brief discussion of the minimum wage as a contributor to inequity, because its influence on the lower portions of the income distribution has been an issue in some other countries.

Demography

The aging of Korea's population is one of the most important changes influencing the country's social policy in the twenty-first century, and the rate of change is among the fastest in the world. The proportion of

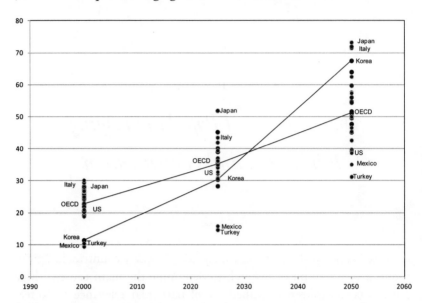

Figure 5.1. Demographic Old-Age Dependency Rate, 2000, 2025, and 2050
Old-age dependency is measured as the ratio of the population age 65 and older to the population age 20 to 64. *Source:* OECD (2007b).

the population over age 65 reached the global average of 7 percent in 2000 and will double to 14 percent by 2018. In contrast, it took more than 100 years for the ratio to rise from 7 to 14 percent in France, 45 years in the United Kingdom, and it will require about 70 years in the United States.

The rapid rate of population aging is the result of large changes in both the fertility rate and life expectancy. The total fertility rate in Korea had fallen to 1.19 by 2008, far below the replacement rate, and the pace of the decline has been very sudden—it exceeded 3 as recently as the 1970s.[1] At the same time, life expectancy in Korea has been increasing at twice the average rate of other OECD countries. The speed of the demographic transition is highlighted in Figure 5.1, which compares the old-age dependency rate of Korea with that of other OECD countries for 2000, 2025, and 2050. Korea's dependency rate is near the bottom of the OECD distribution in 2000 but is projected to rise more rapidly

---

1. The total fertility rate measures the average number of children that would be born per woman if all women lived to the end of their child-bearing years and bore children according to a given fertility rate at each age.

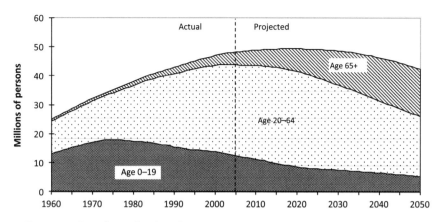

Figure 5.2. Population by Age Groups, 1960–2050
Projections for the Korean population are based on Korea's 2005 population and housing census.
Source: Korea National Statistical Office (2006b).

than the average up to 2025 and then soar to the top of the distribution by 2050.

The changes are also evident in the new projections of the population, shown in Figure 5.2, which are based on the 2005 census. Both the total population and those ages 20 to 64 are projected to reach a peak within the next decade and to decline thereafter. Meanwhile, the population of those under age 20 has been falling continuously since the mid-1970s. In the new projections the old-age dependency rate has been revised up, to more than 75 percent by 2050.

The rapidly aging population can be expected to increase income inequality and poverty in Korea for two reasons. First, there is evidence that as older cohorts come to represent an increasing portion of the total population, inequality increases. Deaton and Paxson (1994, 1997) used micro-survey data from a range of countries to show that the distribution of income within an age cohort expands as the cohort ages. An, Jeon, and Lim (2004) also found that population aging was associated with a worsening of equality in the income distribution, using Gini coefficients reported in the Luxemburg Income Study and data on the population structure from the World Development Indicators (WDI) to construct a panel data set covering seventeen OECD nations and selected years from 1971 to 2000. Second, rates of poverty are particularly high among aged households in Korea because of the limited role of the pension system, and thus an increase in the proportion of aged households can be expected to be associated with greater poverty and therefore increased inequality.

More specific to the case of Korea, Lim and Jeon (2005) used a cohort analysis and Gini decomposition on data obtained from the first six waves of the Korean Labor and Income Panel Study to examine changes in income inequality within age cohorts over time. Consistent with the international analysis, they reported that income inequality increases with the mean age of the household heads. Their results suggest that income inequality both within the older age groups and between older and younger age groups is an important cause of the widening of the income distribution. Similarly, An, Kim, and Jeon (2002) reported that the poverty rate of people age 60 and above was 42.6 percent in 2000, which is more than twice the overall poverty rate of 18 percent. We report a similar result in Chapter 3. However, since much of the poverty problem is associated with the current immaturity of the national pension system in Korea, the situation will gradually improve in future years as more workers qualify for a full retirement pension. Still, as we will discuss in Chapter 6, poverty among the elderly will remain a problem because a large number of irregular workers remain outside the pension system.

The Interaction of Education and Age

In Chapter 2, we showed that most of the increased inequality of overall household incomes can be traced to widening disparities within the wage component. In this respect, Korea's experience is similar to many other industrial economies that have reported a rising level of wage inequality (OECD 2008a, 79–81). However, the detailed patterns of change show some significant differences. In the United States, for example, the post-1990 changes are heavily concentrated in the top half of the earnings distribution, and the range of variation of wage incomes in the bottom half of the distribution has remained unchanged or perhaps even narrowed (Autor, Katz, and Kearney 2005). Korea has the reverse situation in that the increased inequality is most evident in a widening of the differences in the bottom half of the distribution.

Educational attainment and the age composition of the work force are the two dimensions in which the transformation of Korea has been most dramatic. Korea has had one of the world's fastest rates of gain in educational attainment of the work force and, as we have discussed, the age structure of the work force is also changing at a rapid rate. Shifts in the relative demand and supply of skilled versus unskilled workers are particularly popular explanations for changes in the earnings distribution in many countries. In Korea, we observe a positive correlation between changes in the measures of wage inequality and the wage premiums associated with different levels of educational attainment. The period of reduced wage inequality, lasting from the mid-1980s up to the mid-1990s, was marked by a decline in the wage premium for college-educated workers compared with those with a secondary-school degree. The premium has since increased right up to the present (see Figure 2.9). Since the financial crisis, we also observe a very substantial deterioration in the relative earnings of workers who have less than a secondary-level education. These trends are at least suggestive of a major role for education in accounting for the widening wage distribution.

However, the analysis is complicated by the fact that educational attainment and age are inversely correlated in Korea. The rapid gains in educational attainment of younger workers create unusually large disparities in the formal skill levels across different age cohorts of workers. While wage rates normally rise with age because of the relationship between age and experience, the differences in formal education pull in the opposite direction. Therefore, we need to distinguish between the two factors.

We observed that the measures of earnings premiums show considerable difference between the Household Income and Expenditure Survey and the Occupational Wage Survey.[2] In particular, the HIES reports a larger rise in the earnings premium for college-educated workers after the 1997–1998 financial crisis and a much larger deterioration in the relative wage of those with less than a secondary-level education. We attribute these differences to the incomplete coverage of the OWS: it does not survey the public sector or small enterprises and it overrepresents manufacturing at the expense of construction and trade. As a consequence, it excludes a large number of workers at the extremes of the educational distribution, and most important, it excludes large numbers of older workers. Many of the workers missing from the OWS are outside the formal sector of large enterprises. The two surveys also differ in their

---

2. These differences are discussed in Chapter 2 and depicted in Figure 2.9.

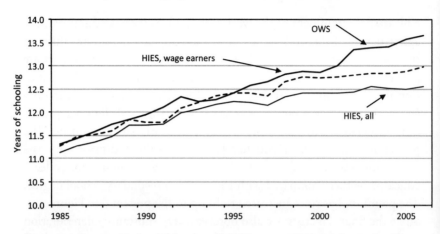

Figure 5.3. Average Years of Schooling: HIES versus OWS (Males Only, All Ages), 1985–2006

The comparisons are limited to male wage earners and, in the case of the HIES, male heads of households. *Source:* Tabulated from HIES (Korea National Statistical Office 2009) and OWS (Ministry of Employment and Labor 2009) data.

estimates of the age distribution of the work force. These age differences contribute to a departure between the HIES and the OWS in their estimates of the trend improvement in the educational attainment of the work force (Figure 5.3). While both surveys show similar gains in educational attainment prior to the mid-1990s, a gap opens up in later years as the OWS reports continued strong growth in educational levels in contrast to the leveling of the gains in the HIES. We attribute this difference to the underrepresentation of older workers in the OWS.[3] In effect, the OWS is increasingly skewed toward younger and better-educated workers.

STATISTICAL ANALYSIS

Our analysis is based on male heads of worker households from the HIES. We treat education and experience (age) as predetermined or

---

3. We are puzzled, however, by the decline of average education levels in the HIES between 1996 and 1997 and the very large jump in 1998 for wage-earner households. The HIES reports ages and educational attainment only for household heads and spouses, but it is not clear why the average would change so substantially in the short run.

exogenous determinants of current earnings and estimate Mincerian regressions in which the log of wage income is related to five educational categories (less than high school, high school degree, some college, college degree, and postgraduate work) and ten five-year age categories. There are 22 regressions covering the individual survey years from 1985 to 2006.

The time series for the coefficients on the education variables are shown in Figure 5.4; they should be interpreted as the difference relative to the average wage of high school graduates. Similar to the results discussed in Chapter 2, the marginal returns to education show several distinct patterns. The most pronounced is the worsening position of workers with less than a high school education. Although their earnings relative to those with a high school degree improved a bit in the late 1980s, the earnings gap widened substantially between 1992 and 2006 before narrowing in 2007–2008. Earnings of those in the three certification levels above the benchmark of a high school degree also indicate a narrowing of the premiums during the first part of the period (roughly 1985 until the financial crisis) and a widening in the years after the crisis. However, the increase in the premiums for those with more than a high school education is not as pronounced as the change in the wage penalty

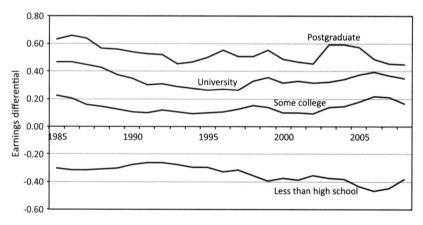

Figure 5.4. Earnings Differentials by Level of Educational Attainment, HIES, 1985–2008
Earnings differentials for male household-head earnings (wage earners only) are measured relative to the earnings of high school graduates. *Source:* Tabulated from the HIES (Korea National Statistical Office 2009).

for those with less than a high school education. Thus, education had a substantial equalizing effect on income in the first half of our period, but it was a source of increased inequality after the crisis. The pattern of widening wage differentials appears to have reversed over the last two years of our survey data, 2007 and 2008, but that is an insufficient period of time to be sure of a change in the trend.

The coefficients on the age variables yield a strongly humped age profile, as average earnings roughly triple between ages 25 and 50 and then decline to half their peak by ages 60 to 65. We observe very little systematic change in the age coefficients over time and do not report them separately. There is, however, a major change in the composition of the work force around the time of the financial crisis. The proportion of heads of households over age 60 who were employed was a steady 60 to 65 percent prior to the crisis but fell sharply to 50 percent by 1989, and it has remained at that lower rate up to the present. Thus, the crisis appears to have translated into a permanent reduction in job opportunities for older workers.

We interpret the residuals from the above Mincerian equations as measures of earnings adjusted for differences in education and age. Figure 5.5A reports the original 90/10 ratios and those based on the predicted and residual values. The measure based on the predicted values identifies movements in the income distribution that can be explained by changes in the age and education composition of the labor force or the coefficients, whereas any movement in the residual inequality measure represents changes in the distribution due to other unidentified factors. It is notable that the residual inequality measure has remained largely free of trend over the period, though it incorporates most of the short-run movements, such as those around the time of the financial crisis. In contrast, the predicted measure captures the U-shaped pattern of change in the actual measure of inequality. Thus, it appears that a combination of changes in education and age can explain both the initial decline in inequality prior to the mid-1990s and its secular rise thereafter. Figure 5.5B shows the actual and residual measures for the 90/50 ratio and the 50/10. Again, the residual measures are largely free of trend, suggesting that education and age effects can account for both the minor U-shaped change in the top half of the distribution and the relatively steady rise in inequality at the bottom. As we would expect, the residual measures account for the short-run variations.

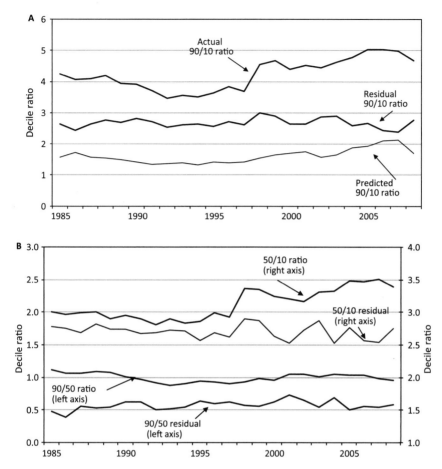

Figure 5.5. Actual and Residual Income Decile Ratios, HIES, 1985–2008
(*A*) Actual, predicted, and residual values for the 90/10 ratio. (*B*) Actual and residual measures for the 90/50 and 50/10 ratios. Male household-head earnings (wage earners only). *Source:* Computed from HIES data (Korea National Statistical Office 2009).

DECOMPOSITION ANALYSIS

An alternative means of accounting for changes in income inequality is a decomposition method outlined by Fields (2003). It identifies the change in earnings inequality in terms of changes in both the quantities (age and education) and their prices (the estimated returns).[4] It also

———

4. We made use of a Stata program constructed by Fiorio and Jenkins (2008) in performing the calculations.

makes it possible to provide a decomposition of the contributions of age and education. Using the same earnings regression specification outlined above, this method calculates the share of inequality attributed to each regressor in the equation, using the coefficient of variation (CV) as a measure of inequality.[5] Any unaccounted-for inequality is listed as a residual component. For ease of explanation, we sum the shares of the education levels and age categories and are left with a time-series decomposition of inequality in Korea according to age, education, and a residual. The results of this decomposition are shown in Figure 5.6.

The top line in the figure shows the level of the coefficient of variation over the period from 1985 to 2008. Its movements are similar to those of the Gini that we reported in Chapter 2. It also shows a gradual decline in inequality up to the mid-1990s, a sharp rise during the 1997–1998 crisis, and a modest upward trend in the 2000s. This is broadly consistent with the pattern of change in the 90/10 decile ratios presented above. However, there is more evidence in this formulation that unidentified residual factors played some role in the decline in inequality up to the mid-1990s and its rise thereafter. The contribution of education narrowed substantially in the late 1980s, consistent with its equalizing effect during that period, but it has increased in subsequent years. Furthermore, the role of individuals' ages has been steadily increasing since the beginning of our sample; accounting for just 4 percent of inequality in 1985, its share had risen to 10 percent in 2006.

The contributions of age and education can each be decomposed further into their major categories. We find that the growing contribution of age to inequality is fully accounted for by the increased proportion of wage earners over the age of 60. We also observe that the narrowing of the contribution of education in the 1980s was mainly the result of the large increase in the number of university graduates, for whom the wage premium narrowed in the late 1980s, but differences in educational attainment have been a source of increased inequality in recent years. There is a similar U-shaped pattern in the contribution of those with less than a high school degree. The education results are similar to the earlier analysis, but the decomposition method is more explicit in high-

---

5. The CV ratio is the ratio of the standard deviation of the distribution to its mean. It is shown in logs for convenience of measuring the contributions, but the pattern of change does not differ from the standard measure based on actual values of earnings.

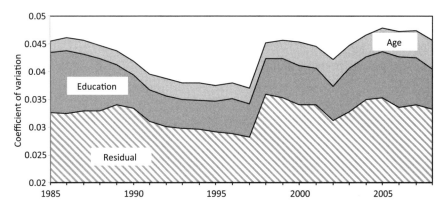

Figure 5.6. Decomposition of Coefficient of Variation by Factor, 1985–2008
Coefficient of variation of male household-head earnings (wage earners only). *Source:* Computed
from HIES data (Korea National Statistical Office 2009).

lighting the importance of changes in the age distribution of the work
force.

ROLE OF EDUCATION

The influence of education on the wage distribution is most easily understood within the context of the relative demand and supply for skilled
versus unskilled labor, where education is the primary determinant of
skill. If we use the proportion of male heads of households (based on the
HIES) with more than a secondary education as a measure of the supply
of skilled workers, it rose sharply from 23 percent in 1985 to 36 percent in
1995, but then slowed to reach only 42 percent in 2005. Similarly, the rate
of decline in the proportion of the work force with less than a high
school degree slowed after the mid-1990s. Alternatively, if the overall
change in skills is measured by the average years of schooling, the rate of
improvement also slowed substantially after 1995 (see Figure 5.3).[6]

If the pace of skill improvement slowed after the mid-1990s in the
face of a hypothesized steady growth in the relative demand for skilled
workers, the result would be a widening out of the distribution of earnings. In effect, though, the rapid buildup of human capital in the years

---

6. The measures of educational attainment accelerated again after 2005, but that
might be influenced by the change in the sample structure in the later years.

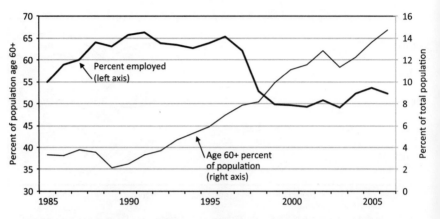

Figure 5.7. Labor Force Participation and Share of Total Population, Age 60 and Older, 1985–2006
Source: Constructed using data on male household heads from the HIES, 1985–2008 (Korea National Statistical Office 2009).

before 1995 exceeded the growth of demand, compressing the wage structure. In the more recent period, the pace of change on the supply side seems to have fallen short of the growth in demand, and the relative price of skills increased.

ROLE OF AGE

The strong role of age in accounting for changes in the wage distribution is the result both of the increasingly humped shape of the age-earnings profile and the rising share of older persons in the work force. As shown in Figure 5.7, the share of male heads of household over the age of 60 has increased fivefold, from 2 to 3 percent in the late 1980s to 15 percent of the total in 2006.[7] The proportion of those men who were employed (including self-employed) averaged 64 percent in the decade prior to the financial crisis, fell abruptly to less than 50 percent in 1999, and has averaged between 50 and 55 percent in recent years. Thus, the financial crisis hit this age category particularly hard, and many have retired or become unemployed.[8] Those who remained in the wage-earner positions also suffered

---

7. Again, these calculations are based on urban worker households with two or more members. We were not able to extend the analysis beyond 2006 because of a change in the information on households by type.

8. The HIES does not distinguish between unemployed and retired.

reduced economic circumstances; the proportion of workers in the lowest wage decile who were age 60 and older rose from an average of only 5 percent in 1985–1989 to 34 percent in 2002–2006, a striking pace of change.

Globalization

In many industrial countries, it has been common to attribute an increase in earnings inequality to globalization. As economies at very disparate levels of development become more closely linked, it is possible that increased trade will result in a widening of earnings among workers of varying skills. Within the more technologically advanced economies, for example, it is possible that expanded trade with countries with large endowments of unskilled labor will lower the wages of unskilled workers in the domestic market and raise the earnings of those at the top of the skill distribution. From that perspective, Korea is oversupplied with highly educated workers compared with the global economy, so an expansion of their opportunities in an increasingly open global market would tend to raise their wages. In contrast, workers with low levels of education are relatively scarce within Korea, but they would face increased competition at the global level, pushing down their wage rates. Thus, the pattern of change in the wage distribution over the past decade is at least consistent with a deepening of Korea's integration with the global economy. In Chapter 4, we also reported a significant correlation between a widening of the income distribution and various measures of cross-border economic activity. Because Korea has not experienced any significant labor migration, it seems to us that global influences on the wage structure must operate through trade. That is the motivation for exploring in greater detail the role of external trade in the increase of inequality. Korea has experienced two distinct periods of strong growth in trade: 1970–1974 and 1994–2008. Total trade (exports plus imports) rose from less than 40 percent of GDP to about 60 percent in the first period, remained relatively stable, and then surged after the financial crisis to reach 107 percent of GDP in 2008. There were generally trade deficits in the years prior to the currency crisis, except for a brief period of surplus in 1984–1989, but Korea has generated consistent export surpluses after 1998.

If we group imports by originating country into three categories, advanced economies, non-fuel-exporting countries, and fuel-exporting countries, we observe that the share accounted for by the advanced economies has slowly declined over the past 30 years, whereas imports from non-oil-exporting developing countries have risen from 3 percent of GDP in 1980 to 14.6 percent in 2008. For example, Chinese imports represented just 0.2 percent of Korean GDP in 1980, and that share grew to more than 8 percent in 2008. We can formalize this analysis by first weighting the exports and imports of each partner country by the ratio of the country's GDP per worker to that of Korea. Thus, countries with a GDP/worker ratio greater than that of Korea will have an increased adjusted measure of trade. We then compute an index of the relative labor costs of trade by computing the sum of the adjusted import/export values relative to the sum of original values for each year. The resulting ratios for both imports and exports are shown in Figure 5.8, where the declining trend of the index indicates a steady expansion of Korea's trade with countries with a lower level of relative wages.[9] Thus, there is at least the potential for increased competition from lower-wage countries.

We can further investigate some of the income implications of expanded trade by examining the patterns of wage growth among industries that differ in their exposure to the global economy, hypothesizing that any influence of trade on the wage distribution should operate through and be most evident in the tradable industries. Using data on the ratio of exports plus imports to domestic production, we classify industries into three categories: internationally tradable, nontradable, and potentially tradable. We use a trade share of 40 percent as the cutoff between tradable and nontradable, and we separate a special category of services (finance, business services, and communications) as potentially tradable (Burtless 2007).[10] This classification, which changes dynamically over time, is matched with the data of the OWS, for which we have measures of earnings by industry of employment.

The results are reported in Figure 5.9. As shown in Figure 5.9A, there is no significant difference between monthly earnings in the tradable

---

9. We made a set of similar calculations using the comparison of the GDP/worker ratio of the trading partner with the GDP/worker ratio of the United States. It yields a very similar pattern of a declining trend in the index of relative wages of Korea's trading partners.

10. Information on trade and production by industry is drawn from the Structural Analysis (STAN) data files compiled by the OECD.

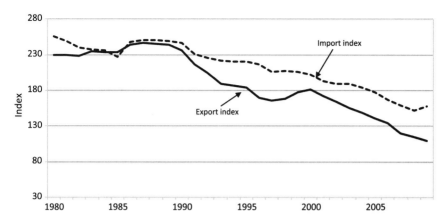

Figure 5.8. Income Composition of Korean Trade, Relative Income per Capita, 1980–2008
Trade is reweighted with GDP per capita of trading partner relative to GDP per capita of Korea.
Source: Constructed with data from Direction of Trade Statistics (International Monetary Fund 2010) and measures of GDP per capita from World Development Indicators (World Bank 2010).

versus nontradable industries. Average earnings are higher in the category of potentially traded services, owing to the employment of individuals with high levels of education. All three series show remarkably similar trends. Standard ratios of earnings in the 90th and 10th deciles within each industrial category are shown in Figure 5.9B. The largest change in inequality is seen within potentially traded services. The categories of tradable and nontradable industries both show some increase in earnings inequality since the mid-1990s, but there is a smaller increase in inequality for tradables.

By themselves, these patterns of change in earnings provide no evidence about the source of the increase in income inequality. In an integrated labor market, relative wage rates would be expected to change in a similar fashion across industries. However, the smaller changes in inequality within the traded industries at least suggest that the initiating forces are not coming from those industries.

Minimum Wage

Korea has had a legal minimum wage since the beginning of 1988. It was gradually expanded from large manufacturing establishments to cover all workers by 2001. There is a lower standard—equal to 90 percent of

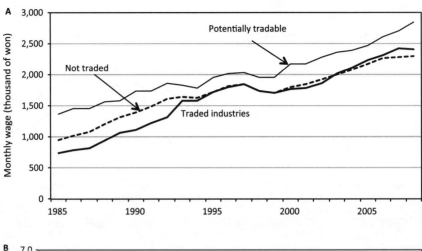

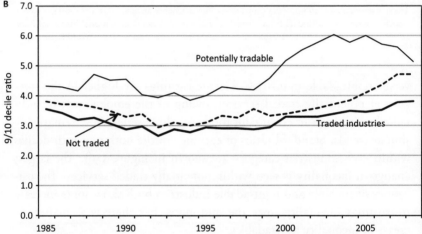

Figure 5.9. Earnings in Traded and Nontraded Industries, 1985–2008
(*A*) Monthly wages indicate average earnings of male workers. (*B*) The decile ratio is the ratio of earnings in the 90th and 10th deciles within each industrial category. Calculations are limited to the earnings of men, and there was a change in the industry classification in 1992–1993.
Source: Constructed from the OWS (Korean Ministry of Labor 2009).

the minimum wage—that applies to workers with less than six months of tenure and those under age eighteen. It is enforced on an hourly basis and excludes overtime and bonus payments. The minimum wage is reported in Figure 5.10 both on an hourly basis (in 2000 prices) and as a percent of the median earnings of male household heads in the HIES.

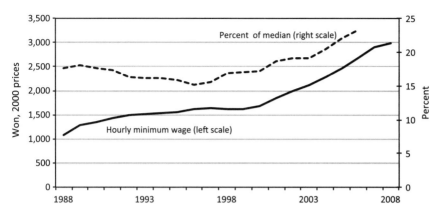

Figure 5.10. Korean Minimum Wage, 1988–2008
The hourly minimum wage, in won, is converted to year-2000 prices using the PCE of the national accounts. The median is the hourly wage multiplied by 160 and expressed as a percent of male head-of-household earnings in the HIES (Korea National Statistical Office 2009).
Source: Korean Ministry of Labor and authors' calculations.

For a few years after its introduction, the minimum failed to keep up with overall wage growth, but it has been rising relative to the median since the financial crisis. The same pattern of change is evident for comparisons to other measures of economywide wages, such as the average wage from the establishment reports. However, the OECD reports that Korea has one of the lowest minimum-wage levels among its member countries.[11] The percent of the mean and median wage rates is comparable to those of the United States and Japan, but well below those of Europe.

It seems implausible that the minimum wage could have had a significant impact on the earnings distribution. It has been rising relative to median earnings over a period when the distribution of earnings has been widening in the bottom half of the distribution. Thus, there is a negative correlation between the ratio of the minimum wage to the median and distributional measures such as the 50/10 ratio. In addition, the minimum wage is only about half that of the earnings associated with the lowest decile of the earnings distribution, well below the level at which it would impact the earnings of many workers.

---

11. Data are available in the OECD Online Employment Database (OECD 2011).

Conclusion

In examining of the role of changes in worker skills and age as explanations for the widening of the wage distribution, we find a strong correlation between changes in educational attainment and the age distribution of the male work force, and the observed increases in wage inequality. In fact, after adjusting for educational attainment and age, we find little evidence of any residual. This is consistent with a simple supply-and-demand model of the labor market in which educational attainment and age are measures of supply-side changes in the work force, and changes in the skill intensity of the demand for workers are assumed to occur at a relatively even rate. The period prior to the mid-1990s was marked by very rapid growth in the relative supply of skilled workers, which helped to compress the wage structure. However, an inevitable slowing of the rate of improvement in educational attainment and an aging of the labor force have both contributed to increased wage inequality in years after the mid-1990s.

We also examined the potential role of globalization by dividing industries into those that produce tradable goods and those that do not. We found that the degree of wage inequality was very similar in the tradable and nontradable industries and that they had changed in a parallel fashion over time; we found no evidence that the change in inequality was more pronounced in those industries that were most exposed to international trade. The increase in inequality was greatest in a group of service-dominated industries that we labeled potentially tradable, but it appears to reflect the high wage within the finance industry and is not directly related to the issue of trade.

Finally, we have not been able to examine fully the distributional effects of the increased bifurcation of the Korean labor market. Regular workers in large firms and those employed in the public sector have traditionally been provided with lifetime employment, protection from dismissal, severance pay, and a wide range of social insurance programs, while workers in smaller firms have generally had a far more tenuous job situation, without the benefits of social insurance coverage. The expansion of the trade union movement after 1987 strengthened social protection for regular workers in the large firms, but also contributed to the growing distinction between regular and nonregular employment. In recent years, even the large firms have increased their reliance on temporary contract workers as a means of avoiding the rigidities of regular employment.

As we will discuss more fully in Chapter 6, there are major deficiencies in the equitable provision of social insurance for nonregular workers. In addition, nonregular workers are paid a lower wage than regular workers (Lee and Jeong 2008). However, we know little about the income, education, and other socioeconomic characteristics of nonregular workers. The HIES has a major design problem in that it does not provide information on the two types of employment equivalent to the classification developed for the annual Supplementary Survey of the Economically Active Population. This is an important area that we have not been able to explore fully because we cannot link type of employment to other socioeconomic characteristics that are known to affect incomes. It is likely that the increased bifurcation of the labor market is a contributor to the growing income inequality, but we could not devise an effective means of evaluating that link.

PART III

The Role of the Public Sector

Until recently, considerations of social equity were not central to the development and conduct of Korean governmental policy. The emphasis was on the promotion of economic growth as the most effective means of improving the general welfare, and in this dimension Korea has been very successful. However, as incomes rose and governance shifted toward a more open democratic structure, Korea experienced a steady expansion of interest in a social welfare system that would assure a broad sharing of the gains from economic growth. Particularly since the financial crisis of 1997–1998, there has been an increased use of the tax and transfer systems to provide a social protection program for those adversely affected by economic developments, and to meet the needs of the aging population. Korea has also sought to improve the quality and efficiency of its publicly provided services.

Social protection systems involve a mixture of redistribution programs that reallocate income from the rich to the poor and insurance programs that are aimed at protecting against adverse outcomes (unemployment and health insurance) or changing life-cycle circumstances (pensions). Historically, Korea has emphasized the latter, and as we shall show, government programs have a surprisingly modest impact on the income distribution. In a recent OECD study of the social tax and transfer systems of member countries, Korea had the lowest rate of public transfers (3 percent) and taxes (8 percent) as shares of the disposable income of working-age households (OECD 2008a, 103). Its transfers to retirees were also far below the average.

In this section, we focus on an evaluation of the distributional aspects of Korea's taxes and its social welfare system. Chapter 6 provides a discussion of the structure of the major public transfer programs and an evaluation of their impact on the distribution of social well-being. In Chapter 7, we provide a description of the income tax system and an assessment of its redistribution aspects. Finally, Chapter 8 considers some proposals for improving the efficacy of the tax and transfer system.

CHAPTER 6

The Role of the Social Welfare System

The most notable attribute of Korea's social welfare system is its small size.[1] Its social welfare programs receive the smallest share of GDP of all of the OECD countries. This is highlighted in Figure 6.1, which compares total public social expenditures as a percent of GDP in Korea with an average for other OECD countries. At 6.4 percent of GDP, Korea's expenditures are only about one-third of the OECD average. While there is an observable tendency for the share of GDP devoted to such expenditures to rise with average incomes, Korea is still far below the norm. Social welfare in Korea receives a smaller share of GDP than programs in the Czech and Slovak Republics, which are close to Korea in income level, and it even appears as an outlier relative to Japan.

Additional details on the composition of social expenditures and their growth over time are provided in Table 6.1. Although the individual programs remain small in a comparative context, their growth generally exceeds that of the OECD average. In a comparative context, the expenditures are particularly small for old-age retirement and family benefits (general poverty alleviation). Yet it is also true that the system has evolved dramatically over the past two decades. Existing programs have been expanded and new programs have been introduced. There are currently

---

1. We have adopted a relatively narrow definition of social welfare to refer to the use of governmental programs to provide economic assistance to people in need. We have tried to include the major transfer programs and significant redistribution elements of the tax system, but we do not examine the provision of education, job training, or housing.

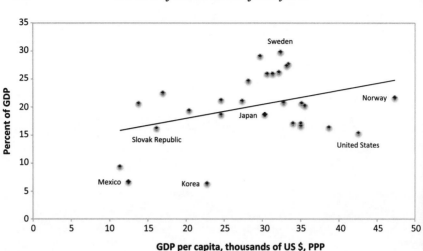

Figure 6.1. Total Social Expenditures as Percent of GDP, OECD Countries, 2005
GDP per capita is expressed in thousands of U.S. dollars; PPP = purchasing power parity.
Source: OECD (2007a) and authors' calculations.

five major social insurance programs: the national pension, national health insurance, unemployment insurance, workers' compensation, and a new program of long-term care insurance for the elderly. In addition, public assistance in the form of cash payments to the poor is provided through the National Basic Livelihood Security System (NBLSS), which was introduced in 2000.

In the decades prior to the financial crisis, government policy was driven by a commitment to a "growth first" policy and the belief that social goals were best achieved by rapid economic growth—a form of trickle-down economics. Placing too much emphasis on distribution was perceived as weakening incentives and the potential for growth and improvements in efficiency. Even today, Korea is very much in a transition stage as it moves away from an informal family-centered system of social protection to state-sponsored programs.

In the following sections, we review the recent changes in the operations of the four largest programs: the national pension, health care, unemployment insurance, and the NBLSS. We then use information from the household surveys to evaluate the distributional effects of these social welfare programs.

Table 6.1. Public Social Expenditures as Percent of GDP: Korea and OECD
Averages, 1990–2005

	1990	1995	2000	2005
Total				
Korea	2.9	3.3	5.0	6.9
OECD	18.1	19.9	19.3	20.5
Old age				
Korea	1.1	1.7	1.9	2.3
OECD	9.2	9.9	9.7	10.0
Health				
Korea	1.6	1.5	2.2	3.2
OECD	4.9	5.2	5.4	6.2
Family benefits				
Korea	0.0	0.1	0.1	0.3
OECD	4.9	5.2	5.4	6.2
Labor market				
Korea	0.0	0.0	0.5	0.3
OECD	1.8	2.3	1.7	1.7
Other				
Korea	0.2	0.1	0.3	0.4
OECD	0.4	0.5	0.5	0.5

Source: OECD (2007a) and authors' calculations.

Note: Old age includes the survivor and disability programs; unemployment insurance is grouped with other labor market programs.

National Pension

Traditionally, Korean society emphasized the role of family and fostered a system of family-oriented care for the elderly; coresidence in two-, three-, and four-generation households was a core element of that system. However, the transition to a modern society has brought a rapid change in the living arrangements of the elderly, as shown in Table 6.2. Although the proportion of households with an elderly member increased by more than a third, from 21 percent in 1996 to 33 percent in 2008, nearly three-fourths of the elderly now live independently of their

Table 6.2. Composition of the Living Arrangements of the Elderly, 1996, 2000, and 2008 (percent of households)

Type of household	1996	2000	2008
No elderly member	79	74	67
Elderly member	21	26	33
Of elderly-member households (%):			
Couple household	34	40	41
Household head unmarried	5	6	6
Single-person household	16	20	29
Aged dependents	44	33	24
Of aged dependents (%):			
Parents		96	84
Grandparents		2	3
Others		2	13

Source: 1996 and 2000 values taken from NSHIE micro-survey data (Korea National Statistical Office 2002); 2008 values are from the HIES micro-survey data (Korea National Statistical Office 2009).
Note: Elderly is defined as 60 years of age and older.

children. As a result, society has been called on to provide new institutions to provide income support for the elderly.

CURRENT PENSION STRUCTURE

Korea's National Pension Service (NPS) was introduced in 1988. The program was gradually expanded from coverage for establishments with ten or more workers to universal coverage for all workers, including the self-employed, in 1999. The contribution rate is currently 9 percent, allocated equally between the employee and employer. It is a partially funded defined-benefit system in which the basic pension amount (BPA) has a two-tier structure, with a flat-rate component tied to the economywide average wage and an earnings-related component that reflects the insured's past contributions.[2] Benefits are adjusted annually for inflation.

---

2. The BPA is determined as: $1.5 \times [A + B] \times (1 + .05 \times n/12)$, where A is the average of the price-indexed national monthly wage in the three years prior to initial benefit

Participants must contribute for a minimum of 10 years, and the BPA is reduced for contribution periods of less than 20 years (by about 50 percent for those retiring with 10 years of contributions) and increased for contribution periods up to 40 years. Concerns about long-run financial insolvency resulted in a scaling back of promised benefits in 1999 and again in 2007. Because benefits are computed on the basis of an average of the individual and the economywide average wages, the benefit system is highly redistributional, raising benefits for low-wage workers. Currently the average BPA is about 50 percent of the average wage for a hypothetical worker with 40 years of contributions, but it will gradually decline to a replacement rate of 40 percent by 2028. There are small upward adjustments for spousal and dependent benefits (including parents) and there is a survivor's benefit equal to about 50 percent of the deceased's BPA. The system also includes a disability program in which the benefit is based on the degree of disability. A full pension is currently paid at age 60, but the retirement age is scheduled to gradually rise to age 65 by 2033.

Since current contributions far exceed benefits, the reserves of the NPS have grown at a rapid rate and were equal to about 25 percent of GDP at the end of 2007. After passage of the National Pension Reform Act of 2007 (National Pension Service 2008), which scaled back benefits, the system's reserves are projected to reach a peak share of 52 percent of GDP in 2035, but to be exhausted by about 2060. The reserves are largely invested in financial assets—allocated among domestic bonds (80 percent), equities (10 percent), and a small foreign component (10 percent). The returns on the fund have been quite variable year to year, but the nominal yield averaged 7.2 percent in 2001–2006.

FUTURE CHALLENGES

Despite the series of recent reforms to the national pension system, Korea still faces several obstacles in developing an effective response to the problems raised by the aging of its population.[3] First, as discussed in Chapter 5, the country is aging at a very dramatic rate. The extreme nature of

---

payment, B is the insured's average wage-indexed monthly wage over the insured's total contribution period, and n is the number of insured years in excess of 20.

3. A most thorough discussion of the basic pension policy issues in an international context is provided by Barr and Diamond (2008).

the drop in the fertility rate to 1.3 implies a very small future working population to provide the revenue base needed to support future pension payments. Such a dramatic demographic transformation rules out a pay-as-you-go pension system because of the heavy burdens that would be placed on future generations of workers. Yet, while the current system incorporates a significant degree of prefunding, it will not be sustainable over the long term without further increases in the rate of contribution.

Second, Korea currently has a severe poverty problem among the elderly. Based on data from the 2006 Household Income and Expenditure Survey, 36 percent of households headed by a person age 65 and older reported having size-adjusted income below the minimum income standard of the NBLSS, compared with just 10.5 percent among all households. Using a poverty standard equal to 40 percent of the median, Moon (2003) reported a relative poverty rate of 49 percent for aged households, compared with 12.6 for all households. In Chapter 3, using an age standard of 60, we reported rates of both absolute and relative poverty among households with an elderly member that are three to four times that of households with no elderly members.

In large part, the high level of poverty is a reflection of the immaturity of the NPS. Currently, only about 20 percent of those over age 65 receive benefits, and those benefits are still quite low owing to the short period of contribution.[4] Reflecting the strong link between past contributions and current benefits, the NPS will not become a major source of income for the elderly until after 2025. Current projections, for example, indicate that only 30 percent of the elderly (age 65 and up) will be receiving benefits from the NPS by 2020.[5]

Third, the coverage of the NPS remains surprisingly low because many workers do not contribute. In mid-2007 the NPS had about 18 million insurants, representing 77 percent of the total employed. Another 5 percent are covered by separate public employee and private school teacher pension programs. However, that still leaves more than 15 percent of the work force outside of the pension programs. More impor-

---

4. Information on benefit recipients and the operation of the Basic Old-Age Pension are drawn from Ministry of Health, Welfare, and Family Affairs (MIHWFA 2008).
5. MIHWFA (2008), 11.

tant, in any given year 25 to 30 percent of the insurants are not active contributors, owing to low reported levels of income (Moon 2008). Much of the problem arises because only about half of the insurants are regular employees in workplaces where the employer takes responsibility to collect and pay both the employee and employer portions of the contribution. Others—the self-employed, part-time workers, and other nonregular workers—are individually insured and account for the bulk of the exempt noncontributors.[6] Low participation is a particular problem among low-income workers, despite the favorable redistribution features of the benefit formula.

Long-Term Solvency   After passage of the 2007 reform bill, new long-term projections of the NPS were prepared and published in late 2008. The projections extend to 2078 and include two alternative scenarios that differ primarily in the assumed fertility rate in future years. In the base scenario, the fertility rate is assumed to slowly rise to 1.28 in 2030 and later years. The alternative incorporates a higher fertility rate of 1.6, but it is still well below the rate required to stabilize the population. The base scenario also assumes life expectancies will continue to rise until 2050 and will be constant thereafter at 83 years for men and 89 for women. On the economic side, real wages and labor productivity are projected to grow at a 3.5 percent annual rate in the early years, before slowing to 2.5 percent in the later years. This is slower than in the past, but it is consistent with a continued convergence of real incomes with the OECD average. Because the labor force begins to decline after 2015, overall GDP growth slows to 0.7 percent per year by the end of the projection period.

The severity of the demographic challenge is most evident in the sharp rise in the system-dependency rate—the ratio of pension recipients to contributors—shown in Figure 6.2.[7] In the base case, the ratio

---

6. It is alleged that the self-employed systematically understate their income in what is effectively a self-assessment system. Since half of any future benefit is based on the economywide wage rate rather than the individual's own earnings history, the net return in the form of future benefits per unit of contribution declines for those with higher earnings, creating an incentive to minimize one's own reported income.

7. Beneficiaries are the sum of retirees, the disabled, and survivors.

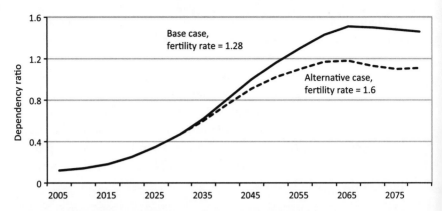

Figure 6.2. Dependency Rate of the National Pension System, 2005–2078
The dependency ratio is computed as the number of beneficiaries per contributor. The base case reflects a fertility rate that slowly rises to 1.28. The alternative assumes a larger increase in the fertility rate to 1.6 after 2010. *Source:* National Pension Fund Institute (2008).

rises from 0.13 in 2008 to an extraordinary 1.5 by 2065. The higher fertility rate incorporated in the alternative scenario does lower the ratio in the later years, but it still peaks at 1.2 recipients per contributor. The system dependency rate is also notably higher than the aged dependency rate—the ratio of persons over age 65 to those age 15 to 64—discussed in Chapter 5. In part this is because of a very gradual increase in the retirement age to 65, and also the continued low coverage ratio, as not all workers contribute to the system in each year.

The projected financial conditions of the fund are shown in Figure 6.3. Most notable is the magnitude of the rise in the cost rate (each year's expenses, or benefit payments, as a percent of taxable incomes), shown in Figure 6.3A. The cost rate is also equivalent to the pay-as-you-go tax rate, if each year's tax were limited to the amount necessary to cover that year's benefit payments. Because the system is still young and most persons have not yet qualified for benefits, the cost rate is currently very low, 3 percent; however, it will rise sharply over the next several decades and peak at an estimated 23 percent of the tax base in 2065. The increase in the cost rate is largely a reflection of the demographic situation, and it highlights the impractical aspect of a pay-as-you-go system for Korea. Due to the extreme nature of the future aging of the population, a pay-as-you-go system would impose drastic costs

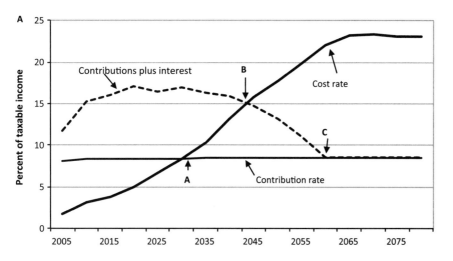

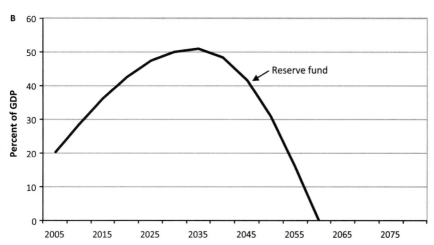

Figure 6.3. Financial Condition of the National Pension System, 2005–2078
(*A*) Income and cost rates for the national pension. (*B*) The pension reserve fund as a percent of GDP. The cost rate equals expenditures divided by the tax base; total income rate equals contributions plus interest, divided by the tax base. *Source:* National Pension Fund Institute (2008).

on future workers and lead to rates of taxation that would be difficult to enforce.[8]

In the projections, the premium contribution rate is held constant at 9 percent. In the early years this yields a substantial annual surplus, which results in a rapid buildup of reserves. Benefit costs will rise to exceed annual premiums by about 2030 (point A in Figure 6.3A), but investment income will enable continued surpluses for another fifteen years (point B). The fund will peak as a share of GDP around 2040 to 2045, and will be rapidly drawn down in subsequent years, with exhaustion by 2060 (Figure 6.3B). Once the fund is exhausted, the contribution rate would have to jump from 9 percent to the cost rate of 2060—that is, 23 percent—to continue to pay benefits on a pay-as-you-go basis. Thus, the system is not sufficient to finance the full level of promised benefits for today's new entrants to the work force.

The system's funding problems can be traced to two fundamental difficulties. First, even after the scaling back of benefits embodied in the 2007 amendment to the pension system, the promised pension cannot be financed with only a 9 percent contribution.[9] A fully funded system would require a contribution rate of about 18 percent, even after full implementation of the 2007 amendments. The high contribution rate is a reflection of the rapid increase in real wages, 2.5 to 3 percent annual growth, which is built into the Korean pension projections. Future benefits are indexed for wage increases up to the time of retirement, but contributions are made on the basis of current wages. Thus, a steep wage-time profile requires a high contribution rate.[10] Second, the reductions in benefits are being phased in on a gradual basis and their effect is further delayed because they apply only to income earned after the date of implementation. Thus, current and near-future retirees will receive large subsidies in the form of benefits much in excess of their contributions. Those legacy costs will be borne by future workers, and they will con-

---

8. A pay-as-you-go system can be sustained in situations in which the age distribution of the population remains relatively constant over time. Korea has the diametric situation, and some degree of funding of future obligations is critical to keeping the costs of the pension system within reasonable bounds.

9. As outlined above, the scaled-back pension calls for a BPA with an average replacement rate of 40 percent on income earned after 2028.

10. If we reduce the projected wage growth to 1.5 percent per year, the fully funded contribution rate declines to about 14 percent.

tinue to grow so long as the contribution rate is maintained below the fully funded rate.

The 2008 report explored the implications of several alternative contribution rates. One approach relies on a partial funding rule that specifies a constant contribution rate that would keep the system in balance to the end of the projection period.[11] In the base projection, subject to a terminal reserve equal to two years of benefit payments, the contribution rate would need to be raised immediately from 9 percent to 12.5 percent. While this constitutes a 30 percent increase in the contribution rate, it remains significantly below the rate associated with a fully funded system. Postponement of the required rate increase will lead to an ever-expanding level of unfunded pension liabilities.

Income Redistribution   The 2007 reforms also addressed the problem of high rates of poverty among the elderly by creating a new Basic Old-Age Pension. It is a means-tested benefit program targeted at persons age 65 and older that is financed out of general revenues.[12] By relying on general funds, it represents a sharp break with the approach underlying the NPS of eligibility based strictly on prior contributions. The baseline level of income was set in 2008 to cover the lower 60 percent of the elderly population and is being expanded to cover 70 percent in 2009 and later years. Eligibility is measured from public records and excludes the income and property of other persons responsible for support (such as children).[13] In 2008, the eligibility standard was a monthly income of 400,000 won for a single person and 640,000 for a couple. That is equal to about 85 percent of the national minimum income standard used in the National Basic Livelihood Security scheme. The benefit amount is targeted to be 5 percent of the average monthly income of NPS recipients.[14]

---

11. The 70-year horizon is roughly consistent with the expected work life plus retirement of a new entrant. Some analysts would suggest the finances should be evaluated with an infinite horizon, because with the 70-year horizon the fund could easily again be out of balance a few years after a corrective action. However, the infinite-horizon calculations may stretch credibility.

12. Details of the program's operation are taken from MIHWFA (2008).

13. Property is converted to income by assuming a 5 percent return.

14. The benefit is scheduled to increase to 10 percent of the income of NPS beneficiaries by 2028.

In 2008, the maximum monthly benefit was 84,000 won for a single person and 134,000 for a couple. The benefit is reduced for those whose postbenefit income would exceed the eligibility standard. In February of 2008, the total number of beneficiaries was nearly two million, with only about one-fourth in couple households, and nearly all received the full benefit amount. Only 100,000 were also recipients of the national pension.

In addition to the impact of the new Basic Old-Age Pension, the NPS itself also has strong distributional effects because half of the individual benefit amount is based on systemwide average earnings and half is determined by the recipients' own earnings history. For example, workers with lifetime earnings that are half of the average receive a benefit that is two-thirds of that received by the average earner. However, this aspect of the NPS will not be an important feature until the system becomes more mature and provides income support to a larger portion of the elderly population. For the near future, poverty among the elderly is concentrated among those who are not eligible for an NPS pension and it is largely a reflection of the continued low coverage rate—particularly among workers in the lower portions of the earnings distribution.

Pension Coverage   The long-term projections do incorporate an assumed modest improvement in the coverage of the pension system, but the failure to achieve universal coverage continues as a major failure of the current system. Without some provision for additional income support, old-age poverty will remain a grievous social problem (see the discussion of poverty in Chapter 3). In fact, the introduction of the Basic Old-Age Pension as part of the 2007 reforms should be seen as recognition that coverage of low-wage nonregular workers will not expand significantly in the near future. In addition, popular options such as conversion to a defined contribution system would appear to worsen the problem of low participation by these same workers. The experience of other countries, such as Chile, suggests that the conversion to a defined-contribution system intensifies the coverage problem among low-wage workers. The lack of pension coverage is closely related to the growth in the share of nonregular workers in the total work force. These workers and the self-employed are responsible for making their own contributions, and they are apparently quite myopic in their evaluation of the future benefits. These problems would become even more severe if the contribution rate were increased to a level more consistent with full-funding of the NPS.

The Basic Old-Age Pension would seem to provide a means of establishing a new first tier of pension coverage that could be easily expanded to address the poverty concerns directly, while leaving the NPS as a funded general pension plan. The Basic Old-Age Pension is means-tested and financed out of the general fund, thus circumventing the problems of limited participation by the self-employed and nonregular workers in the NPS. Continued long-run reliance on the Basic Old-Age Pension with a shift to a consumption-based tax as a source of financing may also be an attractive option. Some have suggested that benefits under the NPS could be then scaled back to bring them more in line with full funding and the current contribution rate. However, large-scale reliance on the Basic Old-Age Pension does increase the long-term concerns because it is an unfunded program. It makes the most sense as a temporary measure aimed at addressing the poverty concerns until a larger number of retirees are receiving full benefits from the NPS. However, that does presume a solution to the problem of limited participation in the NPS.

Health Care

Korea operates a universal public health care system that absorbs a low share of GDP in comparison with the other countries of the OECD. The comparison is summarized for 2008 in Table 6.3. The low public cost is offset in part by a substantial level of private payments, but the combined public and private costs, at 6.5 percent of GDP, place Korea well below the OECD average of 8.8 percent and at less than half of the share of GDP reported for the United States. On the other hand, as shown in the first two columns of Table 6.3, health care costs rise strongly with income and Korea is likely to experience an increase in the share of GDP devoted to health care spending in future years; indeed, that has already been occurring—expenditures were only 4 percent of GDP back in 1995. Still, when combined with the fact that Korea registered the largest gains among the OECD countries in life expectancy between 1960 and 2006, the initial impression is that it is an efficient and effective system.

Table 6.3. International Comparison of Health Expenditures, 2008

	GDP	Health Expenditures per Capita, Thousands of US$	Health Expenditures as Percent of GDP		
			Public	Private	Total
United States	46.9	7.5	7.4%	8.5%	15.9%
France	34.2	3.7	8.7%	2.5%	11.2%
Switzerland	45.5	4.6	6.3%	4.4%	10.7%
Germany	37.2	3.7	8.1%	2.5%	10.6%
Austria	39.8	4.0	8.1%	2.4%	10.5%
Canada	38.9	4.1	7.3%	3.1%	10.4%
Denmark	39.5	3.8	8.4%	1.5%	9.9%
Portugal	25.0	2.4	7.0%	2.8%	9.8%
New Zealand	29.2	2.7	7.9%	1.9%	9.8%
Greece	29.9	2.9	5.9%	3.8%	9.7%
Sweden	39.3	3.5	7.7%	1.7%	9.4%
Iceland	39.0	3.4	7.6%	1.5%	9.1%
Italy	33.3	2.9	7.0%	2.1%	9.1%
Spain	33.2	2.9	6.5%	2.5%	9.0%
Ireland	42.6	3.8	6.7%	2.0%	8.7%
United Kingdom	36.8	3.1	7.2%	1.5%	8.7%
Australia	39.1	3.6	5.8%	2.8%	8.6%
Norway	60.6	5.0	7.2%	1.3%	8.5%
Finland	37.8	3.0	6.2%	2.2%	8.4%
Japan	33.9	2.9	6.6%	1.6%	8.2%
Slovak Republic	23.2	1.8	5.4%	2.6%	8.0%
Hungary	20.7	1.4	5.2%	2.1%	7.3%
Czech Republic	25.8	1.8	5.9%	1.2%	7.1%
Poland	18.1	1.2	5.1%	1.9%	7.0%
Luxembourg	89.7	4.2	5.7%	1.1%	6.8%
Korea	26.9	1.8	3.6%	2.9%	6.5%
Turkey	15.0	0.8	4.4%	1.8%	6.2%
Mexico	15.3	0.9	2.8%	3.1%	5.9%

Source: OECD (2010a).

Note: Expenditures expressed in purchasing-power-parity dollars. Cross-nation expenditures are valued in U.S. dollars using purchasing power parity exchange rates.

Korea introduced mandatory health insurance in 1977 for employees of large corporations and steadily expanded it to cover the full population, achieving universal coverage by 1989 (Song 2009). In 2000, the existing health insurance societies that served different portions of the work force were merged into a single national health insurer.[15] Prior to the single-payer system, rural societies were faced with chronic financial problems because of their older population and unstable incomes—in sharp contrast to the financial situation of urban societies with a younger, wage-based, urban enrollment. Even before consolidation, insurance was based on community rating, with no competition among the health insurance providers.

The system incorporates family-based membership plans on the basis of the employment of the household head. In 2008, the contribution rate was 5.08 percent of wages for those workers covered through their employer, with equal portions paid by the employer and the employee. The provision of insurance for the self-employed and small employment groups is based on a formula that takes account of income, motor vehicles, age, and gender, but the government provides a subsidy equal to about half of the expenditures. The payments of insurants in rural areas, the elderly, and the disabled are also subsidized by the government (NHIC 2007). Payments are monthly but based on income of the prior year. Notably, the contribution does not vary by family size so long as the family members are related by blood.

The national health insurance (NHI) system has much the same problem as the NPS—devising a collection system for the contributions of self-employed and nonregular workers. Although the contribution for employees' health coverage is supposed to be shared by the employer and the employee, 37 percent of the 47 million insurants (who account for 96 percent of the total population) are classified in the self-employed category and are responsible for their full contribution.[16] An annual supplement to the Economically Active Population Survey indicates that only three-fourths of regular workers were covered through their workplace in 2005, and the proportion fell to 36 percent for nonregular workers

---

15. Korea continues to have a small health insurance program for the poor (3 to 5 percent of the population) that is financed with government funds.

16. These data apply to 2007 and are from the website of the National Health Insurance Corporation, http://www.nhic.or.kr/portal/site/eng/.

(Jang 2007, 44). Unlike the NPS, most individuals do participate in the program. Thus, the number of "self-insured" participants is much larger than for the NPS. Apparently, individuals value the immediate benefits of health insurance more highly than the distant benefits of a pension, even though the latter provides a large subsidy to low-income workers. The lack of coverage through the workplace, however, does create problems of verifying the income of insurants.

In contrast to health insurance, the health-care delivery system is largely based on the private provision of services—only 10 percent of hospitals are publicly owned (Kwon 2009) and the government exercises modest regulatory oversight of providers. Patients have almost complete freedom of choice of providers. At present, most providers are reimbursed on a fee-for-service basis, but efforts are being made to switch to a prospective payment system, such as the diagnosis-related group (DRG) system.[17] The 2000 health reforms, however, did separate the prescription of drugs from their dispensing and assigned the latter exclusively to pharmacists. There was some evidence that the old system led to an excessive reliance on drugs, and the reform resulted in protests by physicians and a significant increase in their fees for other services.

The major public complaint against the system is that it covers only a limited range of services and relies on a high level of copayments. As a result, a substantial portion of health care expenditures is paid as out-of-pocket expenses by households. The public share of expenditures has increased considerably since 1990 (Table 6.4) and now finances about 55 percent of the total. Direct payments by households have declined as a share of total outlays over the same period, but at 35 percent, they are high by the standard of other OECD countries. In-patient care is subject to a 20 percent copayment, and the copayment is 40 to 50 percent for outpatient care at hospitals (Song 2009). The copayment is 30 percent for prescription drugs and dental clinics and 20 percent for medical devices, and cosmetic procedures are not covered. There is a ceiling on copayments that varies from two to four million won per year, depending on income, but that is still a significant financial burden for low-income households. In 2008, 76 percent of the population had supplemental

---

17. Thus far, the DRG system has been blocked, except on a voluntary basis, by the opposition of physicians.

Table 6.4. Distribution of Health Care Expenditures by Financial Source, 1990–2008 (percent of total expenditures)

	1990	1995	2000	2005	2008
Government	8.9	8.0	10.1	11.8	12.9
Health insurance	28.3	28.7	35.2	40.3	42.5
Public total	36.3	36.2	45.5	52.1	55.3
Households	58.4	54.6	45.2	38.8	35.0
Private insurance	2.0	2.9	4.6	3.9	4.4
Other	3.3	6.3	4.6	5.1	5.4
Private total	63.7	63.8	54.5	47.9	44.7

Source: OECD (2010a).

private insurance, which helps to finance uninsured care and copayments (OECD 2010a, 102).

The expansion of the insurance system would be expected to raise the flow of health care services to socioeconomic groups that were previously constrained by the large out-of-pocket charges. That is most evident in the increase in the proportion of health care spending directed toward the elderly. In the mid-1980s, health care costs for those age 65 and older were about 120 percent of costs for those age 0 to 64. Relative expenditures on the elderly have increased dramatically over the past two decades and are currently four times higher than the average spent on younger persons (OECD 2010a). In effect, the age pattern of health care spending has become more similar to that of other OECD countries.[18]

In addition, the issue of horizontal equity as defined by "equal treatment of those with equal need" was also examined in a recent paper that compared the experience of Korea with Taiwan and Hong Kong (Lu et al. 2007). The study focused on the distribution of treatments, rather than costs, and it concluded that the Korean system scored high in terms of the equality of access to health care for households of varying income levels. However, based on data from a 1998 health care survey, Ruger and Kim (2007) found that out-of-pocket health care expenditures represented 12.5 percent of income for families in the lowest income

---

18. A similar calculation for the United States yielded a ratio in excess of four in the 1990s, but it has declined slightly in recent years.

quintile, a share that was six times higher than that for families in the top quintile. S.-G. Kim and colleagues (2005) used data from a 2001 survey and reported a similar finding, that out-of-pocket expenditures were a much higher share of income for low-income households and that the outlays of those age 65 and up were twice as high as for younger households. The OECD (2010) report noted that the burden of the copayments contributed to a lower quality of affordable care for low-income households and that the physician shortage was most acute in rural areas.

There is some evidence that reliance on a fee-for-service system and tight controls over fees and the number of new physicians has introduced some inefficiency into the system. Korea has the lowest number of physicians per capita among the OECD countries and they exercise considerable political power over reforms to the system. Physicians have responded to a low rate of reimbursement by scheduling a very high number of office visits. Consultations per physician average 13 per day, about twice the OECD median, and many are minor follow-ups of prior consultations.[19] Similarly, the average length of hospital stays is far in excess of the international norm. The system also makes extensive use of technologies that are not covered by the NHI, like MRIs. The providers have been very resistant to shifting to alternative systems, such as capitation or broad DRGs, that would promote greater emphasis on prevention and the elimination of unnecessary procedures.

A 2003 assessment of the Korean health care system by the OECD also raised some concerns about the quality of the health care (OECD 2003). It pointed to the overreliance on pharmaceuticals, wide variations in clinical practices, and the lack of progress in promoting evidence-based medicine. Korea generally scored below the mean in the OECD quality measures. The Korean Health Insurance Review Agency initiated a quality assessment program in 2005 by selecting areas for priority assessment. It is charged with reviewing the quality and appropriateness of clinical care, but few of the assessments have yet been completed.

A long-term care insurance program, with financing that is separate from the NHI system, was introduced in 2008. It is a response to the rapid aging of the population, but also to changes in family structures that have reduced the availability of family-based care. Korea currently

---

19. See the discussion in OECD (2010), 109–110.

lacks the range of long-term care facilities found in other OECD countries (Kwon 2007). The program, administered by the NHIC, is designed to provide a wide range of in-home and institutional services as well as cash benefits for age-related disabilities. In the first year only 5 percent of the elderly applied, but within two years the rate had risen to 12 percent and about half of those were found to be eligible for assistance. It is still a very small program that can be expected to grow rapidly in future years. It is expected that the program will be financed by the combination of an addition to the existing NHI contribution (60–65 percent), a government contribution (20 percent), and copayments (15–20 percent). The 2010 contribution is set at 0.35 percent of income. Thus far, the planned funding of the program implies a pay-as-you-go approach rather than a funded system.

In many respects, the Korean health care system is a remarkable achievement. It provides universal coverage of the population at a comparatively low cost. The major concerns revolve around the issue of equity. While co-payments appear to have played a critical role in restraining costs and excess utilization, they represent a significant financial burden for low-income households—particularly the elderly. On the other hand, the reliance on a proportionate tax for the basic contribution has made the system affordable for those in the lower portions of the income distribution. The implementation of a cap on copayments is an effective means of providing relief, but it is set at a high level that still constitutes a substantial burden on lower-income households. The program will also face increased financial pressures in future years as the proportion of the population that is elderly increases.

Employment Insurance

Korea was slow to introduce a formal unemployment insurance system. Prior to the financial crisis, the focus was on preventing unemployment rather than ameliorating its effects. In the pre-crisis years of rapid economic growth and job creation, there was neither pressure nor a sense of urgency to create such a program. Instead, Korea relied on a set of job protection rules aimed at preventing employment discharges.

The Employment Insurance System was introduced in 1995, but with extensive exclusions, such as employment units with fewer than 30 workers; new hires over age 60; government officials; private-school teachers;

and temporary, daily, seasonal, and part-time workers. Coverage was expanded to cover a larger proportion of the work force (including regular and nonregular workers) in the aftermath of the financial crisis.[20] In practice, however, coverage continues to be limited, with only 57 percent of wage and salary workers enrolled in 2005 (Grubb, Lee, and Tergeist 2007, 41).

The system has three basic components. The Employment Stabilization Program provides vocational guidance and job placement services, the Job Skill Development Program supports both on-the-job training and subsidies for workers who enroll in vocational training on their own initiative, and the Unemployment Benefits Program provides cash benefits to support the basic living needs of the unemployed as well as their job-search activities. The major budgetary costs are associated with the benefits program.

To be eligible for benefits, a worker must have had insured employment for 180 days out of the previous eighteen months. Benefits are also limited to workers who were involuntarily separated from their job and who are actively seeking reemployment. The benefit is generally set at 50 percent of earnings in the prior job, but it is subject to upper and lower limits. In 2005, 25 percent of the unemployed received a benefit with a replacement rate of 50 percent. The maximum duration of unemployment benefits depends on the period of prior contributions and the applicant's age. For a worker over age 50 who has contributed for 10 years, it is 240 days; workers under the age of 30 are limited to a maximum of 180 days. The average duration of benefits has been 110 to 115 days in recent years. Workers who obtain a job in the first half of their eligibility period receive a reemployment bonus equal to half of their remaining benefits. The contribution rate for the Unemployment Benefits Program is 1.15 percent of wages, excluding performance bonuses. With income and expenditures of about 20 trillion won, the program is very small, accounting for only 0.025 percent of GDP. Despite the expansion of coverage, the Employment Insurance System is largely financed by and provides benefits to employees of large industrial enterprises. Coverage is low for workers in small firms, who frequently have an insufficient contribution history to qualify for benefits.

---

20. The program still excludes workers with fewer than 60 hours per month, government officials, persons age 65 and over, and some private-school employees.

The small size of the Unemployment Benefits Program is evident in the proportion of unemployed workers who receive benefits. D. S. Hwang (2004) estimated the proportion at 15 percent in 2002, well below that of other OECD countries. The low numbers are a reflection of the system's restricted coverage and the short duration of benefits. He also reported that the average annual benefit is only about 15 percent of the average wage, compared with replacement rates in the range of 30 percent and above for other OECD countries. As shown by S. T. Kim (2010), however, the program played a far more important stabilizing role in 2008 compared with 1998 or 2002. The ratio of benefit recipients to the number of unemployed rose from 9 percent in 1998 to 42 percent in 2002 and 109 percent in 2008.[21] In addition, benefit payments increased from a minuscule level in 1998 to 0.1 percent of GDP in 2002 and 0.3 percent in 2008—still a very small program, but one having a rapid pace of expansion.

Public Assistance

The National Basic Livelihood Security System was established in 2000, directly after the financial crisis, as a much broader and reformed version of the prior Livelihood Protection Program. It is a means-tested program that provides cash benefits for housing, living, education, and medical expenses sufficient to raise applicants up to a guaranteed basic standard of living. The basic living standard is set every three years by a consumption survey of low-income households, and it is updated annually with changes in the consumer price index. It includes an adjustment for family size; in 2006 the standard benefit for a family of three was about 30 percent of the median income of an urban wage-earner family.[22] Applicants must demonstrate that the combined value of their income and property is below the living standard and that they do not have children or parents who could provide assistance. Persons who are capable of work must also participate in the self-support program, which is similar

---

21. Because beneficiaries are recorded for each spell of unemployment that they experience, the annual ratio can exceed 100 percent.

22. In 2009, the basic standard for one person was set at 491,000 won. It is increased by 70 percent for the second person and 50 percent for each person beyond two. See as well the discussion in Chapter 3.

to public workfare in that they participate in public works projects in return for their cash benefits.

The Ministry of Health, Welfare, and Family Affairs manages the system, but services are provided through local governments. At the end of 2007, 1.5 million persons were enrolled in the system—3.2 percent of the total population. The aged represent about one-third of the participating households, another third is made up of families with children, and the remainder is split between the disabled and single-parent families. Total expenditures are only about 0.3 percent of GDP, compared with an average in excess of 6 percent for the OECD (see Table 6.1); this represents the largest departure from OECD norms. Over the period from 2002 to 2007, expenditures increased at a 13 percent annual rate and the recipient population, at a 3.5 percent rate.

The self-support program applies to individuals age 18 to 64 who are evaluated and judged capable of working. In extending assistance to households with members who are capable of working, the program is a major departure from the pre-2000 system. Qualified individuals are referred to the public employment service for vocational training and job-search assistance, and others participate in local public works programs. The program continues to have a strong emphasis on work as a condition for receiving benefits.

The NBLSS is a remarkably small program compared with similar programs in other OECD countries. In part, this can be traced to low rates of poverty reported in Korea for individuals of working age. As discussed in Chapter 3, poverty in Korea is dominated by the economic situation of older persons, which we addressed in the discussion of the National Pension Service. However, the low rate of reported poverty can also be traced to the low income standard that Korea uses to measure absolute poverty. Thus, in the cross-national comparisons of the OECD that are based on a relative-income concept, Korea's poverty rate among those of working age is above the average and equal to that of Japan.

Conclusion

Korea's social welfare system has undergone remarkable changes in the past ten years. The basic structures of the programs are not dissimilar to those of other OECD countries, yet Korea still stands out for their modest overall cost when measured as a share of GDP. To some extent this is the result of the developing status of some of the programs, such as the national pension, which will rise in cost as the nation ages. However, in other areas, such as medical care and public assistance, strong cost controls limit the magnitude of benefits financed by the program. Korea has well-designed programs but operates them at a lower level of benefit provision than most other OECD countries.

These modest programs tend to have very little impact on overall income distribution, and they comprise a relatively weak social safety net system. What is striking, in particular, is the degree to which Korea is an outlier among OECD countries in the minimal impact of tax and transfer programs on reducing inequality (see Chapter 7). Furthermore, there is a general problem of low coverage by the national pension and employment insurance programs, particularly among employees of small firms and the self-employed. Looking to the future of the pension fund, this lack of coverage is a major contributor to the severe strains that are a feature of long-term projections. An increase in the contribution rate for the NPS will be imperative in the near future.

There are serious problems of burden sharing for all of the insurance programs based on contributions. Since the contributions are based on ability to pay, it is crucial to have accurate information on incomes. This is not a problem for regular employees whose contributions are managed by their employer. Korea, however, has a large number of workers who are classified as nonregular workers, for whom employers do not arrange for the payment of social contributions. In addition, many people are self-employed in small businesses. The contributions of the self-employed and nonregular workers must be arranged at the individual level, usually through monthly payments. Among such households, the underreporting of income is believed to be severe; in the case of the NPS and the Employment Insurance System, self-employed and nonregular workers often do not contribute at all. This problem might be managed through reliance on income-tax records, but many individuals and businesses are not required to file tax documents. Some have incomes that are below the threshold for the income tax, and among those who do file returns, more than half base their payments on estimated income rather than bookkeeping records. Due to the lack of documentation, it is believed that large numbers of high-earning self-employed professionals pay less tax and contribute less to social insurance than they should.

Table 6.5. Participation in Social Protection Programs, Regular and Nonregular Workers, 2004 and 2008 (percent)

	Regular workers		Nonregular workers	
	2004	2008	2004	2008
Employment insurance	61.5	65.8	36.1	39.2
Medical insurance	73.8	78.0	40.1	41.5
National pension	72.5	77.3	37.5	39.0
Severance payment	67.4	74.5	31.3	35.6
Overtime work payment	65.8	53.5	27.5	28.0
Paid vacations	55.8	65.4	22.2	33.6
Bonuses	58.2	71.2	24.5	27.9

Source: Lee and Eun (2009). Data are drawn from Korea National Statistical Office (2008).

The problem is compounded by labor market legislation that makes a strong distinction between regular and nonregular employment. Regular workers receive extensive protection against dismissal, and that protection is seen as a substitute for employment insurance. It creates strong incentives for firms to avoid hiring regular workers. Nonregular workers can be more easily dismissed, generally have lower wage rates, and are responsible for making their own contributions to the social insurance programs. In 2008, nonregular employment was estimated at 33 percent of the work force.[23] The wide difference among employment classes in their participation in the social protection programs is highlighted in Table 6.5. While it exaggerates the differences—particularly for health insurance—by not including individual payments outside of the workplace, the differences in participation are substantial. The result of the current system is a growing bifurcation of the labor market and of society. We believe that reducing the distinction between regular and nonregular employment would be a critical step toward improving the coverage and equity of the social welfare system.

---

23. Data are from the Supplementary Survey of the Economically Active Population, conducted in August of each year. The 2008 estimate is from Lee and Eun (2009).

CHAPTER 7

The Role of the Tax System

The tax system can be a very powerful tool for altering the distribution of incomes, and the income tax, in particular, is used in many countries to achieve distributional goals. Yet tax systems must be designed to meet a variety of other objectives that may conflict with distributional goals. Here we present a detailed evaluation of the redistributional elements of the Korean tax system, assessing them in terms of both vertical equity and horizontal equity. Vertical equity refers to the progressivity of either a single tax scheme or a whole tax system across taxpayers of different income levels. An income tax scheme can be made more progressive through higher levels of various deductions and exemptions, as well as through a schedule of marginal tax rates that increase with the level of income. Alternatively, a tax system becomes more regressive if it assigns a larger role to a consumption tax than an income tax, because the uniform tax rate levied by a consumption tax, such as the value-added tax or sales tax, places a heavier burden on lower income groups.

Horizontal equity—whether taxpayers of similar incomes pay similar amounts of tax—is also embodied in tax law and tax administration. If the tax law does not cover all income sources, or if it provides loopholes, those with the same income may be taxed differently. In addition, ineffective tax administration can result in more tax evasion as well as higher tax-administration and compliance costs. If, for example, the self-employed are able to evade taxes with a lower probability of being caught than wage earners, this gives rise to horizontal inequity.

Table 7.1. Tax Rates by Categories of Taxable Income, 1998–2010 (percent)

Taxable income (million won)	1998–2001	2002–2004	2005–2007
Below 10M	0	9	8
10M–40M	20	18	17
40M–80M	30	27	26
Above 80M	40	36	35
Taxable income (million won)	2008	2009	2010
Below 12M	8	6	6
12M–46M	17	16	15
46M–88M	26	25	24
Above 88M	35	35	35

Source: Hyun, Jeon, and Lim (2009) and Ministry of Strategy and Finance (2010).

Korean Income Tax System

Three different policy tools largely determine the magnitude of the income tax burden: the tax base, tax credits, and tax rates. The tax base is mostly affected by changes in allowances and deductions, which tend to expand over time in response to political pressures. Changes in tax credits show a similar trend, mainly due to expansions of the tax credit for labor income. Horizontal inequities between labor and self-employed incomes has been a serious problem for Korea's income tax policy, and the government has used the favorable tax credit for labor income to partly solve the problem of horizontal inequity between these two different income sources.

Nominal tax rates are reported in Table 7.1 for the years 1998 to 2010. It is apparent that income tax rates have been reduced over time, suggesting that the burden of the income tax has been reduced. However, the changes in nominal rates do not take into account the effects of the growth of incomes over time, particularly from inflation, which pushes taxpayers into higher marginal tax brackets.[1] This process is highlighted in Table 7.2, which shows the changes in the distribution of taxpayers by category of taxable income over the period from 1998 to 2005.

---

1. Unlike some other countries, Korea does not index, or automatically adjust, its tax system for inflation.

Table 7.2. Distribution of Taxpayers by Taxable Income, 1998–2005 (percent of all taxpayers)

		Taxable income			
	Zero	Less than 10M	10M–40M	40M–80M	More than 80M
1998	14.3	46.6	37.2	2.0	0.0
1999	20.2	40.4	37.2	2.0	0.2
2000	15.2	40.3	40.8	3.3	0.4
2001	12.3	36.8	45.8	4.7	0.5
2002	10.7	36.7	46.9	4.7	1.0
2003	5.7	33.0	49.8	10.6	0.9
2004	5.9	30.2	49.4	13.6	0.9
2005	9.0	24.9	50.1	14.4	1.5

Source: Hyun, Jeon, and Lim (2009).
Note: M = million Korean won.

As incomes have grown, taxpayers have moved into higher tax brackets. For example, the proportion of taxpayers with no taxable income has declined over time, and the number in the highest two income brackets, those with a taxable income of more than 40 million won of taxable income, has risen from about 2 percent in 1998 to almost 16 percent in 2005. Thus, changes in the net tax burden are the result of two conflicting trends: changes in the tax law—changes in tax brackets, lower rates, and more generous allowances—that have reduced tax payments, and a general shift of nominal incomes into higher tax brackets. A full examination of changes in the distributional burden of taxes requires a more detailed analysis based on the distribution of taxpayers' before- and after-tax incomes.[2]

Changes in the distribution of tax payments result from either changes in the deduction and exemption amounts or changes in the income tax bracket associated with specific tax rates. Using the personal exemption and deductions for a family of four, we observe two major changes in the level of tax-exempt income: (1) in 1989, a sharp increase from 2,440,000 won to 4,035,000 won, and (2) an even larger increase in

---

2. Several studies have used micro-level data sets to measure the redistributive effect of the Korean income tax system. Recent examples are those by Hyun and Lim (2005).

1996, from 6,270,000 won to 10,570,000 won. These two increases in the tax-exempt amount gave rise to a more progressive income tax.

Major changes in income brackets and the associated tax rates can also influence progressivity. In 1989 the previous system of sixteen brackets with rates varying between 6 and 55 percent was reduced to eight brackets with rates ranging between 5 and 50 percent. In 1991, the number of brackets was further reduced to five. The 1989 changes were designed to yield a more progressive tax structure, while the 1991 change reduced progressivity. In 1993, the lower limit of the highest income bracket was raised from 50 million won to 64 million, reducing the income tax burden of households in the highest income class.

The most dramatic income tax reform was implemented in 1996. The number of tax brackets was reduced to four, with a broadening of the tax base; the minimum rate was raised from 5 to 10 percent, and the maximum rate was cut to 40 percent. The 1996 reform also introduced the comprehensive taxation of financial income, which played an important role in improving income distribution. The 1996 reforms took great strides in increasing the progressivity of Korea's tax system.

After implementing the comprehensive taxation of financial income during 1996 and 1997, the system reverted to the separate taxation of financial income in 1998.[3] The return to the separate taxation of financial income, together with drastically increased interest rates, was responsible for a major portion of a decline in tax progressivity in 1998. The Korean government then reversed policy again in 1999 by changing the deduction system to increase the general exemption amount, and the comprehensive taxation of financial income was reintroduced in 2001. Tax rates for the lower three brackets were reduced in 2008 and the reduction in the upper-bracket rate was postponed until 2012. A small earned-income tax credit was also introduced in 2008.

PROGRESSIVITY

There are two major approaches to the measurement of tax progressivity (Duclos and Tabi 1996). The first approach measures it in terms of the

---

3. Comprehensive taxation of financial income means the inclusion of financial income in the taxable income, while separate taxation applies a proportional tax rate to the financial income.

shares of the total tax burden borne by different portions of the pretax income distribution (Kakwani 1977). For example, the smaller share of the tax burden borne by the poor, the greater the progressivity of the tax system. The second approach measures progressivity on the basis of the redistributive effect of taxes. For a fixed distribution of pretax incomes, the greater the progressivity of the tax system, the more equal the distribution of after-tax income (see Pechman and Okner 1974; Reynolds and Smolensky 1977).

The Kakwani-type progressivity measure calculates changes in the relative distributions of taxes and income, and in general, it is independent of the scale of taxes. However, the Pechman-Okner progressivity measure looks at overall redistributive effects; the total effects are the product of redistributive effects of one unit of taxes and the total units of taxes. The first element in the Pechman-Okner approach can be interpreted as density. Hence, it is qualitatively equivalent to a Kakwani-type progressivity measure. The second element is the volume of revenues. Therefore, it is quite possible for a tax with low progressivity, when it is measured in terms of the Kakwani-type index of progressivity, to have large redistributive effects (that is, high progressivity measured by the Pechman-Okner approach) when it involves a large volume of revenue.

The effect of tax policy on vertical equity can be measured by comparing the pretax and posttax income distribution. If the posttax inequality is reduced relative to the pretax inequality and the gap between the two measures becomes larger, the redistributive effect of tax policy would be more equalizing. Recently, Kim and An (2000) and Kim and Lim (2000) constructed various indexes of tax progressivity based on pretax and posttax income inequality in Korea using the 1982–1999 Household Income and Expenditure Survey.

The first two columns of Table 7.3 show the pre- and posttax Gini coefficients between 1982 and 1999 as measures of income inequality. The Pechman-Okner (PO) index in the third column is computed as the ratio of the change between the posttax and pretax Gini coefficients over the pretax Gini. The Reynolds-Smolensky (RS) index in column four is the simple difference between the two Ginis. More negative values for the PO or RS index imply that the income tax system has become more progressive. We focus on the changes in progressivity during the times of major change in the tax system discussed above—specifically, 1989, 1991, 1993, 1996, and 1999. The changes in the distributional measures at the

Table 7.3. Changes in Korea's Redistribution Index, 1982–1999

Year	Pretax Gini	Posttax Gini	PO index	RS index
1982	0.324	0.313	−0.034	−0.011
1983	0.321	0.305	−0.050	−0.016
1984	0.313	0.299	−0.045	−0.014
1985	0.315	0.301	−0.047	−0.015
1986	0.312	0.297	−0.048	−0.015
1987	0.306	0.289	−0.055	−0.017
1988	0.297	0.279	−0.061	−0.018
1989	0.314	0.294	−0.065	−0.020
1990	0.292	0.274	−0.064	−0.019
1991	0.290	0.273	−0.059	−0.017
1992	0.285	0.269	−0.055	−0.016
1993	0.287	0.273	−0.051	−0.015
1994	0.294	0.279	−0.051	−0.015
1995	0.299	0.282	−0.055	−0.016
1996	0.302	0.284	−0.059	−0.018
1997	0.293	0.277	−0.055	−0.016
1998	0.329	0.312	−0.053	−0.018
1999	0.324	0.305	−0.060	−0.020

Source: Kim and An (2000) and Kim and Lim (2000).
Note: RS = Reynolds-Smolensky index, computed as the simple change in the pre- to posttax Gini coefficients; PO = Pechman-Okner index, the value of the RS index divided by the pretax Gini coefficient.

time of tax law changes are all in the direction of improvements in equality, yet the after-tax Gini coefficients display the same pattern of change as those computed on a pretax basis. That appears to be due to the fact that the basic tax system is biased toward increasing inequality, unless offset by specific tax actions.

Recently, Hyun and Lim (2009) decomposed the separate impact of each component of Korea's income tax system (tax rate, allowance, deduction, and tax credit) on overall progressivity. They closely followed the prior methodology of international studies by Lambert (1993), Pfähler (1990), and Wagstaff and van Doorslaer (2001), using micro-level data sets of household incomes. In their study, Hyun and Lim used the NHIES from 1991, 1996, and 2000. They found that the very generous levels of allowances and deductions in Korea's tax structure create a surprisingly large gap between economic income and taxable income. This has resulted in a situation in which almost half of taxpayers (47 percent in 2000) pay no income tax. They also find that changes in deductions have had the greatest influence on progressivity, relative to changes in tax rates and allowances. Furthermore, changes in tax credits have consistently reduced the progressivity of the tax system. From their work, we can conclude that policymakers should pay more attention to the effects of changes in tax credit as they influence the progressivity of the income tax system.[4]

Sung (2011) recently studied the progressivity of the personal income tax for the period between 1995 and 2009, using the HIES. He found that the income redistributive effects of the personal income tax have remained almost unchanged throughout the period, with about a 3 percent change between the pre- and posttax Gini coefficients. He also estimated the progressivity of the personal income tax burden using the Kakwani-Poddar-Suits (KPS) index, which is a Kakwani-type progressivity measure. The value of KPS runs from zero for the most progressivity to two for the least progressivity (or, equivalently, the highest regressivity). A unitary value for the KPS indicates that the tax burden is proportional to income.

Table 7.4 shows that the KPS of income tax oscillated around 0.66 with small variations throughout the period considered; this implies that the personal income tax of Korea has been consistently progressive. From these findings, we can conclude that the progressivity of the Korean personal income tax did not change much, even though its structure was not indexed for price changes.

Although many studies have made use of measures of tax progressivity to evaluate the overall tax system, all prior studies have calculated tax progressivity solely in terms of the nominal base (e.g., Kakwani 1977). In other words, little attention has been paid to the direct effects of inflation on tax progressivity. Yet even if the income distribution and the tax structure remain constant, taxpayers will pay more taxes than before

---

4. See also our discussion of Hyun and Lim (2002) and G.-J. Hwang (2004) in Chapter 2.

Table 7.4. Gini Coefficients and KPS Indexes, 1995–2009

Gini coefficients	Gross income (A)	After-income-tax income (B)	(B−A)/A (%)	KPS index
1995	0.243	0.232	−4.3	0.675
1996	0.247	0.238	−3.6	0.690
1997	0.281	0.272	−3.3	0.682
1998	0.311	0.303	−2.7	0.686
1999	0.267	0.259	−3.2	0.683
2000	0.280	0.271	−3.2	0.699
2001	0.272	0.262	−3.8	0.688
2002	0.280	0.271	−3.2	0.681
2003	0.283	0.273	−3.4	0.658
2004	0.289	0.279	−3.4	0.660
2005	0.293	0.283	−3.5	0.661
2006	0.330	0.319	−3.3	0.662
2007	0.333	0.322	−3.5	0.670
2008	0.340	0.328	−3.4	0.667
2009	0.330	0.319	−3.1	0.640

Source: Sung (2011).

Note: KPS = Kakwani-Podar-Suits index, which measures progressivity/regressivity of the tax burden. It ranges from 0 to 2. A value of unity indicates that the burden is proportional to income. If it is greater than 1, the burden is progressive; less than 1, the burden is regressive.

when the system is not adjusted for inflation. Imperfect indexation of the tax structure for price changes induces a welfare cost, suggesting that we need to develop a new evaluation approach that incorporates price changes in measures of tax progressivity. A personal income tax system that is not inflation indexed or only partly indexed tends to lower real values of exemption levels and increase the effective tax rates over time. An increased real tax burden may alter the progressivity of the tax system.

While the Korean tax system is not formally indexed for inflation, frequent tax law changes are believed to have resulted in virtually constant tax progressivity. Until recently, the frequent tax law changes also widened exemption levels, lowering the shares of taxpayers who were taxed with a positive burden. As shown in Figure 7.1, the shares

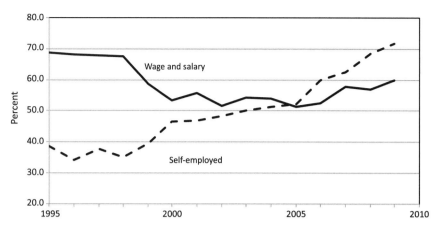

Figure 7.1. Wage and Salary versus Business Income Tax Returns, 1995–2008
The percentage of taxpayers in each category—wage and salary workers and the self-employed
(business owners)—who pay a positive income tax. *Source:* Sung (2011).

decreased dramatically from 68.8 percent in 1995 to 51.3 percent in
2005 for the wage and salary income tax. This shows that frequent
personal-income tax reforms were large enough to overwhelm the inflationary effects, significantly reducing the tax burden for wage and
salary workers.

In contrast, the share of self-employed income-tax payers who were
taxed with positive burden gradually increased from 39 percent in 1995
to 72 percent in 2009, according to the tax return data released by the
National Tax Service (NTS) of Korea (Figure 7.1). For the past two decades, the income tax for the self-employed has not been altered significantly. Because the self-employed tax had long been evaded, the primary purpose of leaving the tax law unchanged for self-employed income
was to enhance the effective business income tax burden by fixing exemption levels at the 1995 level until 2008. The upward trend in the
proportion of taxpayers with positive tax payments, from 39 percent in
1995 to 69 percent in 2009, resulted not only from the inflationary effects of nonindexation, but also from the administrative efforts to raise
tax compliance of the self-employed. The voluntary tax compliance of
the self-employed increased tremendously starting in the early 2000s
when the NTS began to provide taxpayers with tax incentives for credit

card and check card usage and for the immediate electronic reporting of cash receipts.

The changes in the wage and salary income tax and the self-employed (business) income tax were asymmetric. There existed contrastive phenomena, increasing the business income tax base while decreasing the wage and salary income tax base in terms of shares taxed with positive burdens. As a whole, the combined changes in income taxes seem to lead to no overall effects. Therefore, these changes do not seem to be economically significant in terms of the progressivity of their redistribution effects.

INEFFECTIVENESS OF TAX POLICY

We conclude from the available studies that tax policy has not been used significantly in Korea to alter the degree of income inequality (see Table 7.4). The Gini coefficient of after-tax income is only slightly smaller than that of pretax income. The ineffectiveness of tax policy stems in large measure from the high level of deductions and allowances in the Korean income tax system. The large tax exemption enlarges the proportion of nontaxpayers: 50 percent of the population of Korea does not pay taxes. Although Korea uses a relatively progressive income tax rate schedule, its progressivity cannot play any role for those whose income is below the tax-exempt amount. It is unclear why the Korean government does not actively use tax policy to lessen the degree of inequality.

It may be that policymakers are confused by the different concepts of progressivity. While they intended to enlarge the redistributive effects as reflected in the Pechman-Okner concept of progressivity, they actually addressed only the Kakwani type of progressivity through an increased concentration of the personal income tax burden on the high income groups. By expanding the levels of deductions and exemptions, they greatly reduced overall tax revenue, resulting in lowered redistributive effects despite the rise in the Kakwani-type progressivity of the personal income tax. This is shown in Table 7.4 by the decline in the magnitude of difference between the pre- and posttax Gini coefficients in 2008–2009 (less redistribution), while the KPS indexes indicate a small increase in progressivity. Comparing across countries, we see in Table 7.5 that those countries with a higher personal income tax as a percent of

Table 7.5. International Comparison of Redistributive Effects of the Personal Income Tax

	Personal income tax as percent of total tax	Gini coefficients		
		Gross income	After-tax income	Percent change
United States (2005)	35.1	0.45	0.42	−6.5
Japan (2005)	18.3	0.41	0.39	−3.2
United Kingdom (2005–2006)	28.6	0.37	0.34	−8.1
New Zealand (2004)	41.0	0.37	0.35	−5.4
Canada (2001)	36.8	0.36	0.32	−10.9
Australia (1999–2000)	37.8	0.45	0.40	−11.6
Korea (2009)	15.0	0.33	0.32	−3.1

Source: Sung (2011).

Note: After-tax income is defined as gross income minus personal income tax.

total tax tend to have a larger percentage drop in the Gini coefficient going from gross income to after-tax income, although they also tend to have a higher Gini for gross income. We conclude that the small amount of tax revenue obtained from the personal income tax is the primary reason for its ineffectiveness as a redistributive tool.

The unequal tax burden between labor income and self-employed income also contributes to the ineffectiveness of tax policy in Korea. Many studies have shown that wage and salary earners pay more than four times the amount of the self-employed in income tax (Hyun 1996; I. Yoo 1997). Sung (2011) suggests that fundamental inequities exist in the personal income tax burdens between wage-and-salary workers and self-employed workers because of differences in average incomes, degrees of tax compliance, and tax treatments related to income deduction levels. According to his study, the inequity of tax burdens between the two types of income earners mostly originates from differences in tax compliance. He found, however, that the horizontal equity between the self-employed and the wage-and-salary income earners had been ameliorated significantly since the early 2000s through improvements in the tax compliance of the self-employed.

POLICY RECOMMENDATIONS

Tax policy could play an important role in reducing inequality. However, this does not presently occur in Korea. In particular, tax evasion by the self-employed worsens horizontal equity and the large proportion of exempt income limits the effect of a progressive structure of tax rates on vertical equity. Thus, tax policy should focus on reducing tax evasion and broadening the tax base to achieve better income distribution.

The discrepancy in the tax burdens of salaried workers and the self-employed became more serious with the extension of the National Pension Service coverage to the self-employed in urban areas in 2000. With this policy change, the low compliance rate of the self-employed became a more serious obstacle, not only in augmenting tax revenue but also in improving the horizontal equity of tax and social insurance contribution burdens between workers and the self-employed. Thus, tax administration reform should be a major objective of government policy.

As a part of such efforts to reinforce higher voluntary tax compliance among the self-employed, the tax authorities have launched several new programs. Those include the previously mentioned tax incentives for credit card and check card usage and the electronic reporting of cash transactions. Sung (2009) found that the tax compliance rate of the self-employed increased significantly, from 63.1 percent in 2003 to 70.0 percent in 2006. Other studies have suggested additional policy measures that could further reduce the extent of the tax evasion. They agree that the self-employed should rely more on bookkeeping and transaction records, such as receipts, which can provide important evidence for tax audits. They also concluded that special treatment for small businesses, such as the "income standard ratio system" in the income tax law and the special tax payment system in the value-added tax law, should be abandoned. The former allows small businesses to omit a bookkeeping measure of income and instead apply the standard income ratio to their reported sale amount. The latter allows small businesses to report only total sales amounts and to apply the government-recommended value-added ratio to their reported sale amount.

Another weakness in Korea's existing tax system is the relatively lax enforcement of capital gains taxation of financial assets. Under the current system, the equities listed on the Korea Stock Exchange and KOSDAQ, except for those owned by large shareholders, are not subject to capital gains taxation. The securities markets have substantially expanded over the past several years, and the magnitude of capital gains from financial securities will grow in the long run with technological progress and economic growth. Continued tax exemption of capital gains from financial securities could cause substantial tax revenue loss, facilitate tax avoidance by high-income groups, and raise the efficiency cost through the distortion of decision making in investment portfolios.

Finally, as we have noted, the limited redistribution effect of the income tax can be traced largely to its small size and excessive concentration on a few taxpayers. A broadening of the tax base through lower deduction and exemption levels ought to be a major objective of reform. To implement this successfully with little friction, it would also be desirable to introduce inflation indexation into the personal income tax system.

Distributional Consequences of the Tax and Transfer Programs

In most advanced economies, the public tax and transfer programs comprise the primary tool for altering the distribution of income. Governments have often sought to minimize the degree of direct intervention in markets, believing that such interventions could work at cross-purposes to one another and weaken incentives for overall economic growth, but they have felt freer to subsequently modify the outcomes through a system of income taxation and social transfers. Market income is the common term for the receipt of factor incomes from participation in the market economy—prior to the payment of any direct taxes or the receipt of social transfers. In the household surveys, gross income is defined to include transfer receipts, and disposable income is gross income less the payment of direct taxes and contributions to the social programs. Thus, the distributional effect of tax and transfer programs can be evaluated by comparing the difference in measures of income inequality on the basis of market incomes and on the basis of disposable incomes.

We previously noted that social expenditures in Korea are very small, averaging only a third of the average share of GDP reported for the OECD countries. Korea also has a very low level of direct income taxation. Thus, it may be no surprise to find that the difference in the distribution of incomes before and after taxes and transfers in Korea is far

Table 7.6. Differences in Inequality before and after Taxes and Transfers, OECD Countries

	Change in concentration coefficients		
	Market income to disposable income (MY−DY)	*Market income to gross income (MY−GY)*	*Gross income to disposable income (GY−DY)*
Korea	0.02	0.01	0.01
Japan	0.05	0.05	0.00
Austria	0.08	0.05	0.03
United States	0.08	0.04	0.04
Canada	0.10	0.06	0.04
Luxemburg	0.10	0.07	0.03
Finland	0.10	0.06	0.04
OECD average	**0.11**	**0.08**	**0.03**
New Zealand	0.12	0.08	0.04
Norway	0.12	0.09	0.03
Italy	0.12	0.07	0.05
Netherlands	0.12	0.08	0.04
Slovak Republic	0.12	0.09	0.03
France	0.12	0.10	0.02
Great Britain	0.12	0.08	0.04
Germany	0.13	0.09	0.05
Ireland	0.14	0.10	0.04
Australia	0.14	0.10	0.05
Czech Republic	0.15	0.11	0.04
Sweden	0.15	0.12	0.03
Belgium	0.16	0.12	0.04
Denmark	0.16	0.12	0.04

Source: OECD (2008a), 110–112.

Note: A concentration coefficient is similar to a Gini coefficient except individuals are initially ranked by disposable income. Underlying surveys are from the mid-2000s. Gross income includes transfers; disposable income is after taxes.

smaller than in other OECD countries. In fact, if we measure redistribution by the change in the concentration coefficient before and after taxes and transfers (Table 7.6), Korea is a relatively extreme outlier with a magnitude of redistribution that is less than a fifth of the OECD average and only a third of that of Japan.[5] In part, the low degree of redistribution can be attributed to the fact that Korea's level of average income is still below that of the OECD, it maintains a very low rate of unemployment, and it currently has a very young population—all factors that minimize the need for social transfers. But even with those allowances, the extent of redistribution is strikingly limited.

G.-J. Hwang (2004) used NSHIE survey data from 1991, 1996, and 2000 to explore the distributional effects of the tax and transfer programs on the income distribution. He concluded that the social welfare system was of little use in mitigating inequality in market incomes. The programs were small and the public retirement program, in particular, was still in its infancy. In fact, he found that private transfer receipts were more substantial than the public programs. He also pointed out that Korea relies more than most countries on indirect taxes to finance its government programs, leading to a low overall level of direct taxation.

A study by Sung (2009), using the HIES, explored the effect of the tax and transfer programs by computing Gini coefficients for different definitions of income, namely, market-earned income, gross income (inclusive of transfers), disposable income (adjusted for income taxes), and an income measure adjusted for the payment of indirect taxes (Figure 7.2).

In Figure 7.2 the analysis is restricted to a consistent measure of urban households of two or more members. The inequality of market income consistently increases after the financial crisis, from 0.26 in 1999 to 0.29 in 2007, but there is a smaller increase for gross income, largely due to the influence of private transfers. The inequality of disposable income also increased after 2000, but turned down in 2007. In 2007, when the HIES survey included a sample of all households, the Gini coefficient declined from about 0.33 for market-earned incomes to 0.29 for disposable

---

5. The concentration coefficient is computed in the same way as the Gini coefficient, with the only difference being that households are ranked by their equivalized disposable income. See OECD (2008a).

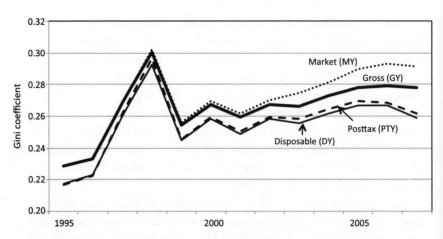

Figure 7.2. Gini Coefficients Based on Equivalized Income, 1995–2007
Data reflect urban-area households with two or more members. GY (gross income) equals market income (MY) plus private transfer income, plus all public pensions and social security cash benefits; DY (disposable income) equals gross income minus income tax, minus other direct taxes, minus social security contributions; PTY (posttax income) equals disposable income minus indirect taxes. *Source:* Sung (2009).

income, with most of the reduction being associated with transfers. Indirect taxes have very little effect on the distribution (Table 7.7). The overall change in the Gini coefficient from market to posttax incomes was a 12.6 percent reduction, of which 8.03 percent was owing to the tax and benefit transfers (although this does not include in-kind benefits).

Sung (2011) updated the results of Sung (2009) using the 2009 HIES. In the more recent study he found that the overall change in the Gini from market to final incomes was a 19.4 percent reduction, from 0.36 to 0.29; of this, 14.9 percent was from the tax and benefit transfers. Thus their redistributive effects had grown larger over time. This was mainly because of recent large increases in cash and in-kind benefits, while the redistributive effects of the personal income tax remained almost unchanged.

Sung (2009) also examined the effects of the tax and transfer programs on his measure of the absolute poverty rate in the HIES. Again, he computed the poverty rate for the different definitions of income. He reports a sharp reduction in the poverty rate as he moves from market-earned income to disposable income, but most of the reduction is accounted for by private transfer payments (Table 7.8). In 2007, the poverty

Table 7.7. Redistributive Effects Based on Rates of Change in Gini Coefficients, 2007 and 2009

	2007		2009	
	Gini	Percent change	Gini	Percent change
Market income	0.327	—	0.360	—
plus private transfer income equals:				
Private income	0.313	−4.5	0.344	−4.5
plus public pensions equals:				
Gross income version 1	0.312	−0.3	0.336	−2.5
plus other social security cash benefits equals:				
Gross income version 2	0.305	−2.4	0.330	−1.8
minus income tax equals:				
Disposable income version 1	0.290	−4.7	0.319	−3.0
minus other taxes and social security contributions equals:				
Disposable income version 2	0.286	−1.1	0.315	−1.1
minus indirect taxes equals:				
After-tax income	0.288	0.6	0.315	−0.2
plus in-kind benefits equals:				
Final income	—	—	0.293	−6.3

Source: Sung (2009, 2011).
Note: Redistributive effects are percentage changes of adjacent Gini coefficients.

rate declines from 5.2 percent for private income, defined as market income inclusive of private transfers, to 2.4 percent for gross income after including government transfers and 2.7 percent for disposable income.

We have extended the results from the NSHIE by using the 2006, 2007, and 2008 expanded version of the HIES, which now includes single-person households and those living in rural areas. This version of the survey also provides summary estimates of incomes for households with a self-employed or unemployed head, even though it does not provide the same detail on income sources as is obtained from households

Table 7.8. Absolute Poverty Rates, 1995–2007

	Market income (MY)	Private income (PY)	Gross income (GY)	Disposable income (DY)
1995[a]	2.24	1.69	1.69	2.09
1996[a]	1.53	1.03	1.03	1.25
1997[a]	6.06	5.42	5.42	6.07
1998	12.60	11.77	11.54	12.68
1999	4.07	3.58	3.31	3.82
2000	2.98	2.42	2.12	2.71
2001	2.10	1.77	1.52	1.74
2002	2.17	1.52	1.24	1.98
2003	6.19	3.20	1.67	2.05
2004	6.50	3.46	1.73	1.90
2005	7.46	4.16	2.11	2.41
2006	10.92	5.24	2.14	2.67
2007	10.88	5.23	2.39	2.71

Source: Sung (2009).

Note: PY (private income) equals MY (market income) plus private transfer income; GY (gross income) equals PY plus public pensions plus other public transfer income; DY (disposable income) equals GY minus income tax minus other direct taxes.

[a] In 1995–1997, PY and GY cannot be fully distinguished in the HIES data sets.

with a working head.[6] That analysis is shown in Table 7.9 for 1996, 2000, and an average of 2006–2008.[7] In each survey, households are distributed by quintiles of gross income—inclusive of transfers, but before taxes and social insurance contributions. The average magnitude of the transfers and contributions to the social programs is shown in the far right column. First, the increase in inequality between 1996 and 2000 is readily apparent in the decline in the share of both gross income and disposable income that is attributed to the two lowest quintiles. However, there is very little change between 2000 and 2006–2008. Second,

---

6. As discussed in the section on poverty measures, we have used the annual averages of the monthly incomes from the 2006, 2007, and 2008 HIES to increase comparability with the earlier NSHIEs.

7. The numbers for 2006, 2007, and 2008 were very similar, and thus the average provides an accurate summary for the three years.

Table 7.9. Taxes, Transfers, and the Distribution of Income, 1996, 2000, and 2006–2008

	Income quintiles (percent of total)					Mean income (thousands of won)
	1st	2nd	3rd	4th	5th	
1996						
Gross income	6.5	13.0	17.8	23.4	39.2	23,917
Direct transfer	15.3	18.0	17.0	21.1	28.7	186
Indirect transfer	31.5	15.9	13.8	16.3	22.5	1,005
Direct taxes	4.9	7.6	13.0	19.9	54.6	617
Pension	2.4	10.6	17.7	27.0	42.3	201
Social insurance	8.9	15.9	20.1	23.1	32.1	221
Medical insurance	9.3	16.0	20.0	22.8	31.9	209
Disposable income	6.6	13.1	17.9	23.5	38.9	22,879
Consumption	9.9	15.9	18.9	23.1	32.2	15,060
Medical expenditure	12.6	17.9	20.4	21.8	27.3	725
2000						
Gross income	5.0	11.3	16.5	23.0	44.1	26,532
Direct transfer	19.1	18.7	19.4	17.2	25.5	478
Indirect transfer	23.8	18.8	19.3	17.9	20.1	1,281
Direct taxes	2.8	6.7	12.4	21.9	56.1	1,044
Pension	2.3	9.0	16.1	26.6	46.0	553
Social insurance	6.5	13.6	17.9	24.4	37.7	451
Medical insurance	7.0	13.9	18.0	24.1	37.0	406
Disposable income	5.1	11.6	16.7	22.9	43.7	24,484
Consumption	9.6	15.3	19.1	23.5	32.5	17,513
Medical expenditure	15.9	16.7	18.7	21.2	27.5	787
2006–2008 average						
Gross income	3.6	10.7	17.3	25.0	43.4	31,675
Direct transfer	19.5	22.3	22.8	15.0	20.5	1,242
Indirect transfer	18.6	18.6	16.6	18.6	27.7	1,950
Direct taxes	2.4	4.3	8.9	19.1	65.4	987
Pension	1.9	7.6	16.0	27.8	46.8	815
Social insurance	5.1	11.3	18.2	25.1	40.1	716
Medical insurance	5.5	11.7	18.4	25.0	39.4	664
Disposable income	3.7	8.5	12.9	17.9	29.8	29,156
Consumption	8.4	14.1	19.2	24.5	33.8	23,550
Medical expenditure	13.4	16.2	18.5	21.5	30.0	1,267

Source: Authors' calculations, based on the 1996 and 2000 NSHIE (Korea National Statistical Office 2002) and the 2006–2008 HIES (Korea National Statistical Office 2009).

Note: Data exclude farm and fishery households. The HIES data are annualized averages of monthly income and expenditure responses. The NSHIE responses are annual values.

as reported in the OECD analysis, the tax and transfer programs have very little effect on the overall income distribution. In fact, indirect (private) transfers comprise the largest and most redistributive item.[8]

On the tax side, the share of direct taxes paid by the lowest two quintiles is about half their share of gross income, implying a progressive tax structure, but the small size of the tax suggests that it does not have a substantial effect on the overall distribution of after-tax incomes. In the survey, it is also shown as declining in size between 2000 and 2006–2008. The problem of avoidance of contributions to the national pension program is also apparent in the low share being contributed by households in the lowest quintiles. This is a major concern for the future, in light of the favorable return available to low-income workers. It also contrasts with the distribution of the health insurance contribution, which is much more proportionate to income. Apparently, low-income households perceive the advantages of having health insurance coverage, but either they are not cognizant of the long-term benefits of participation in the retirement program or they have a very high discount rate. It is also evident that out-of-pocket health expenses—the copayment and uncovered expenses—represent a more substantial burden for households in the lower portion of the income distribution. Furthermore, it is noteworthy that health expenditures by all households increased sharply between 2000 and 2006–2008.

Overall, we interpret the results in Table 7.9 as indicating a very minor effect of the tax and transfer programs on the overall income distribution. They also seem to suggest a smaller role for these programs than was obtained in the analysis of Sung (2009). One reason for the small effect of the transfers is that the public pension plays a small role in redistribution, owing to its immaturity and narrow coverage. The income tax is highly progressive, but its effect is also limited because of its small size.

Tax policy is generally viewed as a useful tool for income redistribution. However, the redistributive effects are typically larger for fiscal expenditures than for taxes. An international comparison of the redistributive effects is shown in Table 7.10. Because distributions of in-kind benefits are not available for all countries, only cash benefits are consid-

---

8. In the Korean surveys, direct transfers are largely public and indirect are largely private.

Table 7.10. International Comparison of Redistributive Effects of Taxes and Cash Benefits (percent change in Gini coefficient)

	Cash benefits	Taxes	Cash benefits plus taxes
Canada	17.1	8.9	26.0
New Zealand	14.0	4.7	18.6
Japan	22.9	2.5	25.4
United Kingdom	26.9	7.7	34.6
United States	9.3	5.9	15.2
Korea	4.3	4.1	8.4

Source: Sung and Park (2011).

Note: The redistributive effects are measured by tax- and benefit-induced percentage changes in Gini coefficients.

ered. Of the six countries illustrated, Korea has the lowest redistributive effects both in taxes and in benefits. Another important feature is that no country shows that the redistributive effects of taxes were larger than those of fiscal expenditures (cash benefits) and, except for Korea, the gaps in redistributive effects between the two factors were quite large.

Conclusion

Why are the redistributive effects of cash benefits much larger than those of taxes? The most probable answer is that, with cash benefits, governments have a greater ability to target benefit programs for specific subpopulations. While it is not easy to select for certain taxpayers, it is easier to limit benefit programs to those who are poor or distinguishable by age.

In this sense, we may draw a couple of policy implications from the international comparison. The first is that Korea is still an outlier in the relative size of its redistributive programs. Some of this will change naturally over time without the need to expand the programs, as the benefit systems mature and the population ages. On the tax side, though, an increased role will not emerge without reform of the basic system.

CHAPTER 8

Improving the Efficacy of
Redistributive Policies

Most industrial facilities in Korea were destroyed during the Korean War and production dropped to nearly zero in the 1950s. Adhering to a principle of growth first and distribution second, government policies in the 1960s concentrated on economic expansion, forgoing any agenda toward social welfare under the assumption that increasing incomes through growth would do more to raise the general welfare level. Many Korean citizens were plunged into a state of absolute poverty by the war, and without any government programs, they had to rely heavily on foreign aid organizations for support. While basic elements of a social welfare system were introduced during the 1960s and 1970s, the coverage was often restricted to the employees of large firms, or the benefits were small.

The demand for welfare programs surged in the late 1980s following Korea's social democratization and a period of extremely rapid economic growth. The country's absolute poverty rate of 40.9 percent in 1965 declined to 23 percent in 1970 and 4.5 percent in 1984 (Suh and Yeon 1986). Contrary to the government's previous focus on unemployment and poverty, the welfare reforms of the 1980s emphasized improvements in the quality of life. Health insurance was extended to the full population, and with the introduction of the national pension in 1988, social insurance became the central focus in an expanded network of welfare programs.

The financial crisis of 1997 forced a new stage in the development of Korea's welfare system. The crisis brought the first increase in the size of the poverty class since the start of industrialization in Korea. As discussed in Chapter 3 and shown in Table 3.3, the absolute poverty rate rose dramatically, from 3.8 percent in 1996 to 6.9 percent in 2000, and it has remained at an elevated level since. Despite the changes that have occurred since the crisis, poverty is still a significant problem—especially among single-person, rural, self-employed, and elderly households. Although a system of employment insurance and the National Basic Livelihood Security System had been established to address concerns about poverty, the financial crisis of 1997 resulted in demands for new and expanded programs to resolve the worsening distribution of incomes in the first decade of the twenty-first century.

The desire for a further expansion of the welfare programs comes from a mixture of two concerns. In the short term, people want programs aimed at mitigating the high unemployment and poverty rates that resulted from the restructuring of the Korean economy after the financial crisis. In the longer term, Koreans are increasingly focused on an improved quality of life, especially around issues associated with the rapid pace of population aging.

The global economic crisis in 2008 added to the pressures on the welfare system, intensifying the short-term need to address unemployment and poverty. There is a concern, however, about future growth in these programs. Policy measures designed to address short-term welfare needs should not become permanent systems, but because welfare systems have inflexible expenses, it is hard to abolish them or to reduce expenditures once they have been established. Short-term welfare policies often continue to burden national budgets in future periods because of the difficulty of ending them.

Two major policy areas are involved in satisfying welfare concerns: tax policy and welfare policy. Various tax policies and welfare programs can be designed for enhancing the redistributive function. As discussed in Chapters 6 and 7, however, tax and welfare policy in Korea have both been shown to play only weak roles in achieving the redistribution objectives. This motivates the proposals for tax and welfare reforms.

Tax Reforms

Tax policy is often used to achieve distribution objectives. However, as discussed in Chapter 7, its redistributive effect is limited in Korea. While the income tax does have a progressive structure, its total size is too small to have a significant redistributive impact. The primary problem is the small tax base, a result of high levels of deductions and exemptions. Sung (2009) reported that, as a result of the deductions allowed, only a small proportion of income earners actually had positive tax payments and average effective rates of taxation were low. He also showed that tax evasion, especially among the self-employed, is another source of the deterioration in the redistributive effects of the tax. Thus, there are two clear changes that could augment the redistributive effects of the personal income tax: broaden the base and reduce evasion.

Even with reform and expansion of the income tax to increase redistribution, there will still be a desire to expand the welfare programs on the expenditure side. Considering the aging population, widening income inequality, and poverty problems, even a reformed income tax would not be a sufficient source of additional revenue to address all those needs. Therefore, an expansion of the value-added tax (VAT) would be a good candidate for a complementary revenue source. Unlike most developed Western countries, where VAT burdens are quite regressive, the VAT in Korea is more proportional to income, according to Sung (2011), because of its broad base. Furthermore, the current VAT rate is only 10 percent, compared with 15 to 25 percent in most OECD countries. These considerations suggest that Korea could increase revenue and finance a large portion of the future costs of welfare programs by raising the VAT rate.

Current Status of the Welfare Budget

The expansion of the social guarantee system has also greatly increased the share of welfare expenditures in the government budget. As of 2009, Korea's welfare budget was about 75 trillion won, approximately 26 percent of total expenditures by the central government. During the period from 2004 to 2009, welfare expenditures increased by an average annual rate of 19 percent. Excluding housing sector expenditures (which were added into the welfare budget in 2006), the rate of increase is still 13 percent. That corresponds to two or three times the average annual increase in total expenditures by the central government, 7.7 percent, during the same period. (See Table 8.1.)

The rapid population aging in Korea plays a major role in that expansion. As discussed in Chapter 5, the total fertility rate decreased to 1.08

Table 8.1. Annual Welfare Budget, 2004–2009 (billions of won)

	2004	2007	2009	Annual increase
Welfare budget	3,236	6,139	7,459	19%
Percent of total expenditure	17%	26%	26%	
Welfare budget, excluding housing	3,236	4,742	5,957	13%
Percent of total expenditure	17%	20%	21%	
Social welfare budget	2,800	5,610	6,772	20%
Social welfare, excluding housing	2,800	4,213	5,271	14%
National basic livelihood	383	658	714	14%
Low-income support	87	91	105	7%
Public pension	1,398	1,900	2,382	11%
Nursing women's subsidy	46	122	193	34%
Seniors and youths	—	75	325	73%
Labor	657	1,043	1,176	13%
Merit	231	297	336	8%
General	—	27	39	32%
Housing	—	1,397	1,502	4%
Health	436	529	687	10%
Health, medical service	46	99	145	29%
Health insurance	378	414	520	7%
Food product safety	11	17	21	14%
Total expenditure (trillion won)	196.2	238.4	284.5	8%

Source: Ministry of Strategy and Finance (2010).

Note: The annual increases in budgets for low-income support, seniors and youths, and general social welfare are averages for 2005–2008. Low-income support in 2004 is the sum of three sectors (low-income support, seniors and youths, and general). Housing has been classified as social welfare since 2006.

in 2005, reaching the world's lowest level. As a result, the youth dependency ratio decreased from 0.78 per adult of working age in 1970 to 0.17 in 2005. Meanwhile, the old-age (over age 65) dependency ratio increased from 0.06 in 1970 to 0.13 in 2005, and it is projected to reach 0.7 in 2050.

The structure of the welfare budget will continue to increase welfare expenses in the future. A high ratio of mandatory expenses results from legal requisites such as livelihood benefits under the NBLSS. According to Park and Lee (2008), mandatory expenses take up about 89 percent of the 2008 budget of the Ministry of Health, Welfare and Family Affairs. These expenditures will automatically expand in future years because of population aging. The high share of mandatory spending also implies that the welfare budget would be severely strained by new welfare demands that might arise because of domestic and international changes such as economic slowdowns, low birth rates, or an aging society.

The Effectiveness of Welfare Policy

The expansion of the social insurance and public assistance systems over the past 40 years has left Korea with a very diverse set of social welfare programs, and since the 1997 financial crisis, the number of recipients of various social guarantees has grown dramatically. However, the rapid introduction of these programs, with insufficient testing of their practical efficacy, has led to problems. To begin with, they were introduced with insufficient administrative infrastructures. For example, Korea has no system to ensure the accurate measurement of income, and the unlawful receipt of benefits under NBLSS is still a significant problem. Also, despite the programs' large budgets, their effectiveness in terms of benefits versus costs is continually questioned.

As discussed in Chapter 7, the improvement of Korea's income distribution induced by taxes and welfare programs is very slight (Sung 2009). The Gini coefficient computed after adding public and private transfer incomes and subtracting various taxes is only slightly reduced. The effect of social guarantees, such as the livelihood benefits under the NBLSS, is even smaller than the effect of the income tax. Welfare policies also have had little impact on the nation's poverty rate (Sung 2009). Poverty reduction through public transfers was only 16 percent in 2007.[1] This is unfortunate, because spending on these programs has rapidly increased since 2000.

We evaluate the programs' efficiency, in terms of their use of resources and their practical efficacy, with the concept of target efficiency. Target efficiency is reflected in a set of indexes that measure how much of the

---

1. Social guarantees also include cash allowances for funerals (paid by the health insurance union or corporate employers) and transportation subsidies for seniors, in addition to basic livelihood benefits. Thus, the poverty improvement from Korea's livelihood benefits may be slightly lower than the measured effect.

benefits from the various welfare programs goes to the intended recipients. Target efficiency can be classified into vertical and horizontal target efficiency (Haveman 1997). Vertical target efficiency refers to the ratio of the benefits from the program received by the members of the target group relative to the benefits received by everyone—that is, the extent to which the target group benefits. Horizontal target efficiency measures the proportion of members of the target group who actually receive benefits from the program—benefits received relative to needs.

An and Jeon (2003) used models of Beckerman (1979) and Weisbrod (1970) with Korean labor panel data to analyze target efficiency of public transfer expenditures during the period from 1998 to 2000. They evaluated whether the efficiency of public transfers was improved through the introduction of the NBLSS. First, using the Beckerman model, they constructed three indexes: vertical expenditure efficiency, the ratio of excessive expense, and poverty reduction efficiency. Vertical expenditure efficiency measures the share of total benefit payments that go to households that were poor in the absence of the program. This index shows the degree of concentration of transfer income in poverty households, and it declined from 77 percent in 1998 to 65 percent in both 1999 and 2000. The excessive expense ratio is expressed as the ratio of payments to households whose income exceeded the poverty line to total allowances paid to poor households, the primary targets of public transfer. This ratio grew from 2.8 percent in 1998 to 5.5 percent in 1999 and 8.1 percent in 2000. Last, poverty reduction efficiency is shown as the proportion of total program payments that go to households that were still classified as poor after receiving benefits; this index decreased from 75 percent in 1998 to 61 percent in 1999 and 60 percent in 2000. While the government increased its resources for fighting poverty after the foreign exchange crisis, there was no improvement in efficiency prior to the introduction of the NBLSS in 2000.

Using a set of target efficiency measures proposed by Weisbrod (1970), we find that receiving households rose as a proportion of all households from 11.8 percent in 1998 to 13.0 percent in 1999 and 14.4 percent in 2000. In this process, the share of receiving households among poor households also escalated, from 26.5 percent in 1998 to 33.8 percent in 2000. However, there was no change in the proportion of poor households among all receiving households, which was 61.1 percent in 1998, 62.0 percent in 1999, and 61.8 percent in 2000. That is, the target efficiency of the public transfers, as measured by the concepts of both Beckerman and Weisbrod, hardly changed during the process of introducing NBLSS after the foreign exchange crisis.

We extended the analysis of An and Jeon (2003) to the 2006 and 2007 family survey data (the Household Income and Expenditure Survey), to measure the target efficiency of welfare transfers for all national families (including the self-employed) with one or more members. The HIES provides less detail about individual transfer programs, but it does report public transfer payments, distinguishing between pensions and other social welfare programs.[2] We find the vertical efficiency of the non-pension welfare payments was only 0.543 in 2006 and 0.508 in 2007. In other words, the ratio of welfare transfers that went to households in poverty was slightly higher than 50 percent. The excessive expense ratio of other social guarantees was 0.174 in 2006 and 0.198 in 2007, signifying that the proportion of payments that went to households above the poverty line was substantial. And the poverty reduction efficiency of the other welfare transfers was 0.449 in 2006 and 0.407 in 2007, denoting that the percentage of transfer income used to reduce poverty was slightly higher than 40 percent.

Calculating target efficiency using the model of Weisbrod (1970), the ratio of recipients of other welfare payments among all households was 32.5 percent in 2006 and 34.4 percent in 2007. The ratio of poor households receiving those payments was 67.8 percent in 2006 and 72.5 percent in 2007. In addition, the proportion of nonpoverty households receiving benefits was 26.3 percent in 2006 and 27.8 percent in 2007. Lastly, the proportion of households receiving benefits that were poor was 31.0 percent in 2006 and 31.2 percent in 2007. The conclusion is similar to that with the Beckman model: the programs are not very efficient in targeting on the problem of poverty.

There are limitations to the direct comparison of the results from the 1998–2000 Korean labor panel data and the 2006–2007 family survey data. Within the Korean labor panel data, payments for poverty reduction are distinguished from other public transfer expenses. In contrast, social welfare transfers in the family survey combine poverty expenses and nonpoverty expenses. Accordingly, our estimate of the share of

---

2. We exclude pension payments, which do not have a specific focus on poverty reduction.

households in poverty among welfare recipients is lower using the family survey data.

Still, the analysis shows that the efficiency of NBLSS is extremely low. For example, about 50 percent of transfers are paid to nonpoverty households. Even after acknowledging that public transfers other than livelihood benefits are included in "other social payments," 50 percent is very large. A large number of poor households are not receiving necessary support while households not in poverty are receiving unnecessary support. A method of preventing unlawful receipt of benefits must be implemented, with an accurate examination of income levels. The system must also ascertain whether there are households that are unable to receive support despite their need. We conclude that high priority should be given to efforts to increase the poverty reduction efficiency of Korea's welfare programs.

Increasing Target Efficiency and Emphasizing Program Evaluation

Once welfare programs are introduced, they tend to be inflexible; it is difficult to abolish them or reduce their cost. Therefore the government should carefully evaluate the efficiency of programs prior to their introduction. The concept of target efficiency provides a useful framework for that evaluation. Currently, however, the evaluation of welfare policies is conducted primarily by individual researchers and there is a lack of systematic government studies. In addition, existing studies mainly focus on understanding such phenomena as the poverty improvement and redistribution effects of welfare spending. Reviews of program effectiveness and efficiency relative to cost are still insufficient. Researchers studying welfare policies should develop their methods and data to serve the objectives of a broader evaluation.

Specific steps toward constructing a standardized evaluation system for welfare policies include the establishment of an evaluation organization within the Ministry of Health, Welfare, and Family Affairs; reinforcement of the role of external evaluators; and development of the data infrastructure required to support the evaluation program. A pre- and postevaluation system for social welfare programs requires that a responsible body develop, collect, and analyze data. The installation of an organization in the Ministry of Health, Welfare, and Family Affairs similar to the Office of the Assistant Secretary for Planning and Evaluation (ASPE) under the U.S. Department of Health and Human Services could be highly useful. ASPE is charged with such tasks as policy research and development, policy adjustment, developing legislation, strategic planning, and economic analysis.

To construct an external evaluation system for welfare programs, Korea should strengthen the role of the National Assembly by emphasizing analysis and evaluation of major national projects as a main responsibility of the National Assembly's Budget Office, which has the same function as the Congressional Budget Office in the United States. Since effectiveness and efficiency should be part of an accounting analysis of program usage and nonusage, the accounting office could also serve as an external evaluator of government projects. In the United States, the General Accountability Office performs the role of analyzing projects of the executive branch departments, and those evaluation studies represent more than half of its workload. In Korea, the government should emphasize the importance of performance audits as a function of the accounting office. Since there could be difficulties in coordinating with the National Assembly because the accounting office is an executive-branch agency, the accounting audit and work inspection could remain as duties of the accounting office, and the National Assembly could take on the evaluation and performance work.

Initially an evaluation program should focus on developing evaluation methodologies and collecting the required data. Experimenting with alternative program designs could also be useful in evaluating the effects of specific policies prior to their general introduction. Through research to pinpoint potential problems in program execution, Korea could develop more cost-effective and efficient social welfare systems.

The evaluation methods will be dependent on proper data to measure various effects, such as the contribution of rehabilitation programs to poverty reduction. In-depth investigation with respect to the demographics of welfare-fund recipients, and follow-up surveys after they exit the welfare program, would provide a clearer picture of the advantages and downfalls of specific measures.

Finally, programs that provide support on the basis of eligibility criteria must have the tools to properly investigate the income and property levels of potential recipients. For example, in the NBLSS there is no reliable way to determine the income of recipients because the livelihood benefits are provided as the difference between a cash allowance standard and self-reported income. Most recipients work in unlisted sectors, further obscuring the accurate calculation of their income level. Since recipients include irregular workers (such as the self-employed, temporary workers, daily workers, and part-time workers), their income cannot be precisely determined for the purpose of assigning social insurance and income taxes. Data processed by government-related institutions are often inaccurate or contain large discrepancies.

We conclude that Korea could improve its welfare delivery system by installing an administrative institution for welfare. This organization could review program management and the enforcement of NBLSS rules, currently enforced by local town offices and other general welfare agencies. Segmentation and professionalization would improve the productivity of those government agencies. A system to coordinate the new institution's efforts with data from the National Tax Office would also greatly improve the operation of the welfare programs.

Individual welfare projects run by local government entities should be connected to welfare institutions of the central government agencies—such as the Ministry of Labor; the Ministry of Education, Science, and Technology; and the Ministry of Patriots and Veterans Affairs—so that their work is processed consistently. By establishing administrative networks at an early stage, the welfare organizations will be able to devote more of their work force to the management of recipients' needs, budget reformation, and execution plans for reducing poverty.

The government should make consistent efforts to supply, maintain, and develop its welfare resources. Financial support, as well as the efficient design and operation of welfare policies, will improve the practical efficacy of these programs, but only if the necessary budget is accurately calculated and there are sufficient resources. Welfare policies introduced without sufficient consideration of budget conditions will be ineffective. It is necessary to remove overlapping and extravagant expenses within the social welfare sector and to review the possibility of reducing expenses through the unification of programs.

Beyond reform of the welfare programs, Korea can create a path out of poverty by reforming the educational system, providing job training, and offering reemployment education. As discussed by An and Jeon (2008), inequality in educational background is directly linked to inequality in income level. Since such linkage occurs both within generations and between different generations, reforms of the educational system and employment policies are critical to improving the income distribution structure and reducing poverty in Korea. These actions will help prevent superfluous welfare budget expenses while satisfying real needs. The introduction of universal taxation on financial income and taxation on gains from stock transfers would also help improve equality and secure financial resources.

The Principles of Social Welfare Funding

Increasing the funding for the social welfare programs is an important and urgent task in Korea, which faces rapid population aging and thus rising demand for poverty alleviation among the elderly. Four steps should be considered for raising and fairly distributing social welfare funds.

EVALUATING THE EFFICIENCY OF WELFARE PROGRAMS

Evaluating current welfare programs in terms of their target efficiency, as we discussed, enables us to identify which programs spend more than is actually needed to achieve program goals. On the basis of results from target efficiency assessments, it is possible to allocate the welfare budget more effectively among various welfare programs, to close loopholes or correct drawbacks in each program, and eventually to save on the welfare budget as a whole. However, while the efforts to evaluate the current system in terms of target efficiency can lead to more effective spending, it does not increase the overall budget for the programs, so these efforts need to be accompanied by additional action to increase welfare funds.

IMPROVING THE OVERALL STRUCTURE OF GOVERNMENT EXPENDITURES

As we discussed earlier, welfare expenditures in Korea constitute a small but rapidly growing share of government expenditures, and that share will need to continue to grow in future years. This means that competition between the welfare budget and other objectives of government will intensify. The government will need to continually reassess the overall budget allocation and search for lower-priority areas that can be cut, given both the prevailing economic and social environment and citizens' demand for corresponding public goods.

OBTAINING SUPPORT FROM RELATED POLICIES

Unequal distribution of income and wealth is a key factor precipitating the demand for welfare. The more unequal the distribution of income or wealth in a society, the greater the demand for welfare benefits from the poor and other welfare recipients, because with high wealth inequality, relative poverty becomes a larger issue than absolute poverty. The demand for welfare can be reduced by aligning welfare and other policies, such as education and tax policy, so that benefits allocated through those channels help to reduce welfare demand overall. Education subsidies or job-training coupons for low-income earners, for example, can reduce the demand for direct welfare payments by helping individuals obtain employment.

Furthermore, much of the problem of poverty is concentrated among the elderly, many of whom are forced to retire early from regular employment with large firms and then seek reemployment as irregular workers, or become self-employed. While the actual retirement age in Korea is closer to age 68, many workers leave their main occupation at age 54 to 57. Then they may spend ten to fourteen years in nonstandard employment, with limited income and often no coverage under the National Pension Service. Because many Korean companies have traditionally paid their workers based on seniority, not on performance, they are reluctant to reemploy retired workers because of their high cost.[3] Roughly 30 percent of workers over age 50 are self-employed, compared with less than 15 percent of younger workers, and a majority of those older workers who are employed are irregular workers.

Efforts to reduce the discrimination between standard and nonstandard workers in terms of coverage of social welfare programs and other fringe benefits would help ensure at least minimal retirement incomes and reduce the incentives for irregular employment in lieu of regular employment. The government could do more to ensure that social insurance coverage is extended to all forms of employment and that employers are held responsible for ensuring the payment of the required social insurance contributions. Enterprises should be encouraged to

---

3. The link between poverty and age is discussed more fully in Chapter 3, and the roles of age and nonstandard employment in the worsening of the income distribution are discussed in Chapter 5.

eliminate job termination at a specific age and to substitute more flexible wage programs based on performance rather than seniority. All of these measures would help alleviate the central problem of high poverty rates among the elderly, while relieving some of the pressure on the NLBSS.

SYNCHRONIZING WELFARE POLICY WITH OTHER POLICIES

Welfare policy can operate more effectively when it is synchronized with other policies. Therefore, the welfare system needs to be closely coordinated with the labor policy and tax administrations. The task of investigating true income becomes particularly important because the administration of welfare, labor, and tax policies all rely on accurate measurement of the income of the self-employed. That measurement can be conducted more effectively by the tax administration, and its findings should be made available to the administrators of labor and welfare policy. Similarly, the Earned Income Tax Credit, introduced in 2008, requires coordination with the welfare system to avoid unnecessary expenditures.

Conclusion

Korea's economy continues to grow at impressive rates, but it faces a series of major challenges in ensuring an equitable distribution of the benefits of that growth and dealing with the rapid aging of its population. In our analysis, we conclude that there has been a significant worsening of the income distribution in Korea that has become more pronounced since the 1997–1998 financial crisis. This widening of the income distribution can be largely traced to interaction effects between age and education. In the early years of Korea's growth, a strong expansion of education contributed to compressing the wage structure by accelerating the supply of skilled workers and maintaining a relatively equal distribution of wages. The slowing of the rate of improvement in educational attainment in recent years and an aging of the labor force have both led to increased wage inequality that is particularly noticeable in the bottom portions of the income distribution. We found no evidence that the growing inequality could be related to the increased interaction of Korea's economy with global markets.

At the same time, Korea has developed a full range of welfare programs, similar in structure to those of other OECD countries, that are designed to moderate income inequities. Korea's current programs, however, which stand out for their relatively low cost and lack of major effect on the distribution of incomes, comprise a relatively weak social safety net. While the programs are generally well designed, there are major gaps in coverage owing to the ease with which workers can avoid making the required contributions. In addition, programs like the national pension system are still in a transitional phase and have not yet had a significant impact on beneficiaries. The difficulty of enforcing contributions has added to the problems with the Korean labor markets, as workers are increasingly divided between those with regular employment and full access to the social welfare programs and those with irregular employment and limited access.

We also find that the Korean tax system makes only a minimal contribution to reducing income inequality. Large numbers of income earners are exempt from the system, and it is plagued with serious problems of tax avoidance by the self-employed. Therefore, the broadening of the tax base through lower deductions and exemption levels and increased compliance ought to be major objectives of reform. In addition, greater attention needs to be paid to keeping the focus of transfer programs on households with low income.

References

Adelman, Irma, and Cynthia Morris. 1973. *Economic Growth and Social Equity in Developing Countries*. Stanford, CA: Stanford University Press.

Ahluwalia, Montek. 1976a. "Income Distribution and Development: Some Stylized Facts." *American Economic Review* 66, no. 2, 128–135.

———. 1976b. "Inequality, Poverty and Development." *Journal of Development Economics* 3, no. 4, 307–342.

Ahn, Joyup. 2004. "Nonstandard Employment Arrangements in Korea: What Have We Learned?" Working paper, Korea Labor Institute, Seoul.

Ahn, Kookshin. 1997. "Trends in and Determinants of Income Distribution in Korea." *Journal of Economic Development* 22, no. 2 (December): 27–56.

Ahn, Kookshin, and Daemo Kim. 1987. *Korea's Income Distribution, Its Determinants and People's Consciousness about Distribution Problems*. Seoul: Chung-Ang University Press (in Korean).

Alesina, Alberto, and Dani Rodrik. 1994. "Distributive Politics and Economic Growth." *Quarterly Journal of Economics* 109, no. 2, 465–490.

An, Chong-Bum. 2003. "The Kuznets U-Hypothesis Revisited for the New Korean Economic Development Model." *Korean Economic Review* 51, no. 3, 5–30 (in Korean).

An, Chong-Bum, Cheol-hee Kim, and Seung Hoon Jeon. 2002. "Interdependence of Poverty and Unemployment and Welfare Policy Effectiveness." *Korean Journal of Labor Economics* 25, 75–95 (in Korean).

An, Chong-Bum, and Seung Hoon Jeon. 2003. "Evaluation of the National Basic Livelihood Security System." Paper presented at the Annual Conference of the Korean Association of Public Finance (Fall).

———. 2008. "Intergenerational Transfer of Educational Achievement and Household Income." *Public Economics Research* 1, no. 1 (in Korean).

An, Chong-Bum, Seung-Hoon Jeon, and Byung-In Lim. 2004. "Population Aging and Its Effect on Inequality: An Extended Empirical Study of Kuznets' Inverted-U Hypothesis." Paper presented at the 2004 KDI-KAEA Joint Conference, Current Economic Issues of Korea.

Autor, David, Lawrence Katz, and Melissa Kearney. 2005. "Trends in U.S. Wage Inequality: Re-Assessing the Revisionists." Harvard Institute of Economic Research Discussion Paper 2095, Harvard University.

Bank of Korea. 2010. National Accounts, http://ecos.bok.or.kr/EIndex_en.jsp.

Barr, Nicholas, and Peter Diamond. 2008. *Reforming Pensions: Principles and Policy Choices.* New York: Oxford University Press.

Beckerman, Wilfred. 1979. "The Impact of Income Maintenance Payments on Poverty in Britain 1975." *Economic Journal* 89, no. 354, 261–279.

Birdsall, Nancy, David Ross, and Richard Sabot. 1995. "Inequality and Growth Reconsidered: Lessons from East Asia." *World Bank Economic Review* 9, no. 3, 477–508.

Bradbury, Kathleen, and Jane Katz. 2009. "Trends in U.S. Family Income Mobility, 1967–2004," Federal Reserve Bank of Boston Working Paper 09-7.

British Broadcasting Corporation (BBC). 2008. "BBC World Service Poll," 7 February, http://www.worldpublicopinion.org/pipa/pdf/feb08/BBCEcon_Feb08_rpt.pdf.

Burtless, Gary. 1999. "Effects of Growing Wage Disparities and Changing Family Composition on the U.S. Income Distribution." *European Economic Review* 43, 853–865.

———. 2007. "Globalization and Income Polarization in Rich Countries." Issues in Economic Policy 5, Economic Studies Program, Brookings Institution, April. Available at http://www.brookings.edu/papers/2007/04useco nomics_burtless.aspx.

Cameron, Lisa, J. Malcolm Dowling, and Christopher Worswick. 2001. "Education and Labor Market Participation of Women in Asia: Evidence from Five Countries." *Economic Development and Cultural Change* 49, no. 3, 459–477.

Choi, Kang-Shik. 1996. "The Impact of Shifts in Supply of College Graduates: Repercussion of Educational Reform in Korea." *Economics of Education Review* 15, no. 1, 1–9 (in Korean).

Choi, Kyungsoo. 2003. "Measuring and Explaining Income Inequality in Korea." Mimeo, Korea Development Institute (July). Available at http://www.eadn.org/reports/iwebfiles/i05.pdf.

Choo, Hakchung. 1982. *Income Distribution and Its Determinants in Korea,* vol. 2. Seoul: Korea Development Institute.

———. 1993. "Income Distribution and Distributive Equity in Korea." In Lawrence B. Kraus and Fun-Ko Park, eds., *Social Issues in Korea: Korean and American Perspectives,* 335–360. Seoul: Korea Development Institute.

Choo, Hakchung, and Joohyun Yoon. 1984. "The Calculation of Income Distribution and Cause of Income Fluctuation in 1982. *KDI Journal of Economic Policy* 6, no. 1 (in Korean).

Deaton, Angus, and Christina Paxson. 1994. "Intertemporal Choice and Inequality." *Journal of Political Economy* 102, no. 3, 437–467.

————. 1997. "The Effects of Economic and Population Growth on National Saving and Inequality." *Demography* 34, no. 1, 97–114.

Duclos, Jean-Yves, and Martin Tabi. 1996. "The Measurement of Progressivity, with an Application to Canada." *Canadian Journal of Economics* 29, Special Issue: Part 1, 165–170.

Fields, Gary S. 2003. "Accounting for Income Inequality and Its Change: A New Method, with Application to the Distribution of Earnings in the United States." *Research in Labor Economics* 22, 1–38.

Fields, Gary S., and Gyeongjoon Yoo. 2000. "Falling Labor Income Inequality in Korea's Economic Growth: Patterns and Underlying Causes." *Review of Income and Wealth* 46, no. 2, 139–159.

Fiorio, Carlo V., and Stephen P. Jenkins. 2008. "INEQRBD: Stata Module to Calculate Regression-Based Inequality Decomposition." Statistical Software Components, S456960, Department of Economics, Boston College (revised 8 December 2008).

Grubb, David, Jae-Kap Lee, and Peter Tergeist. 2007. "Addressing Labour Market Duality in Korea." OECD Social, Employment and Migration Working Paper No. 61, Organization for Economic Cooperation and Development, Paris.

Haveman, Robert. 1997. *Poverty Research: The Great Society and the Social Sciences.* Madison: University of Wisconsin Press, 1997.

Hwang, Deok Soon. 2004. "Unemployment Benefits." In Wonduck Lee, ed., *Labor in Korea: 1987–2002,* 601–626. Seoul: Korea Labor Institute.

Hwang, Gyu-Jin. 2004. "The Mechanism of Income Distribution: The Case of South Korea." *Social Policy and Society* 3, no. 3, 243–252.

Hyun, Jin Kwon. 1996. "The Distributional Effect of Taxes in Korea: Empirical Evidence by Using 1991 Household Data." Working Paper 96-05, Korea Institute of Public Finance, December.

Hyun, Jin Kwon, Seung-Hoon Jeon, and Byung-In Lim. 2009. "The Discrepancy between Statutory Tax and Real Tax Burden: The Case of Korea." *Journal of the Korean Economy* 10, no. 1, 81–92.

Hyun, Jin Kwon, and Sukhoon Kang. 1998. "International Comparison of Income Distribution in Korea." *Korean Economic Review* 46, no. 3 (in Korean).

Hyun, Jin Kwon, and Byung-In Lim. 2002. "Income Distribution in Korea: Empirical Evidence from OECD Guidelines." *Korean Economic Review* 18, no. 2, 315–329.

————. 2005. "Redistributive Effect of Korea's Income Tax: Equity Decomposition." *Applied Economics Letters* 12, no. 3, 195–198.

International Monetary Fund. 2010. Direction of Trade Statistics. Available at http://elibrary-data.imf.org/.

Jang, Sinchul. 2007. "The Unification of the Social Insurance Contribution Collection System in Korea." OECD Social, Employment and Migration Working Paper No. 55, Organization for Economic Cooperation and Development, Paris.

Jung, Gwangsu. 2000. "A Study of Korean Urban Households: Demographic Characteristics, Long-Term Trends, and Post–Economic Crisis Changes in Income Inequality." Research report, Korea Development Institute, December (in Korean).

Kakwani, Nannuk C. 1977. "Measurement of Tax Progressivity: An International Comparison." *Economic Journal* 87, 71–80.

Kaldor, Nicholas. 1978. "Capital Accumulation and Economic Growth." In Nicholas Kaldor, ed., *Further Essays on Economic Theory*, 1–53. New York: Holmes and Meier Publishers.

Kang, Byung-Goo, and Myeong-Su Yun. 2003. "Changes in Korean Wage Inequality 1980–2000." Paper presented at the World Institute for Development Economics Research Conference on Inequality, Poverty and Human Well-being, Helsinki, May.

Kim, Dae-Il, and Robert H. Topel. 1995. "Labor Markets and Economic Growth: Lessons from Korea's Industrialization, 1970–1990." In Richard B. Freeman and Lawrence F. Katz, eds., *Differences and Changes in Wage Structures*, 227–264. Chicago: University of Chicago Press.

Kim, June-Dong, and Byung-In Lim. 2000. "Tax Equality and After-Tax Income Inequality in Korea." *Korean Journal of Public Economics* 5, no. 1, 3–31 (in Korean).

Kim, Sung-Gyeong, Seung-Hum Yu, Woong-Sub Park, and Woo-Jin Chung. 2005. "Out-of-Pocket Health Expenditures by Non-elderly and Elderly Persons in Korea." *Journal of Preventive Medicine and Public Health* 38, no. 4, 408–414.

Kim, Sung Teak. 2010. "Korea's Unemployment Insurance in the 1998 Asian Financial Crisis and Adjustments in the 2008 Global Financial Crisis." Working Paper 214, Asian Development Bank Institute, Tokyo, May.

Kim, Yun Young, and Chong-Bum An. 2000. "Income Inequality, Tax Progressivity, and Welfare." Paper presented at 56th Congress of the International Institute of Public Finance, August.

Korea Labor Institute. 2007. Korean Labor and Income Panel Study (KLIPS), 1998–2006: Wave 1–9 (M1194V1).

Korea National Statistical Office. 1988. *Social Indicators in Korea.* Seoul: Kyŏngje Kihoegwŏn.

———. 1997. *Social Indicators in Korea.* Seoul: Kyŏngje Kihoegwŏn.

———. 2002. National Survey of Household Income and Expenditure (NSHIE). Micro-data set, 2000 and prior years.

———. 2006a. *Changes of Business Cycle Index and Setting Base Cycle Period.* Korea National Statistical Office, Daejeon (in Korean).

———. 2006b. *Population Projections (2001–2050).* Available at http://kostat.go .kr/portal/english/surveyOutlines/1/9/index.static.

———. 2008. *Supplement to the Survey of the Economically Active Population.*

———. 2009. Household Income and Expenditure Survey (HIES). Micro-data set, 2008 and prior years.

———. 2010. *Annual Report on the Consumer Price Index.* Available at: http:// kosis.kr/eng/database/database_001000.jsp?listid=F&subtitle=Price.

Kuznets, Simon. 1955. "Economic Growth and Income Inequality." *American Economic Review* 45, no. 1, 1–28.

Kwack, Sung Yeung, and Young Sun Lee. 2007. "The Distribution and Polarization of Income in Korea, 1965–2005: A Historical Analysis." *Journal of Economic Development* 32, no. 2, 1–39.

Kwon, Soonman. 2007. "Future of Long-Term Care Financing for the Elderly in Korea." *Journal of Aging and Social Policy* 20, 119–136.

———. 2009. "Thirty Years of National Health Insurance in South Korea: Lessons for Achieving Universal Health Care Coverage." *Health Policy and Planning* 24, 63–71.

Lambert, Peter. 1993. "Inequality Reduction through the Income Tax." *Econometrica*, n.s., 60, no. 239, 357–365.

Lee, Byoung Hoon, and Soo Mi Eun. 2009. "Labor Politics of Employment Protection Legislation for Non-regular Workers in South Korea." Paper presented at Conference on Regulating for Decent Work: Innovative Labour Regulation in a Turbulent World, International Labor Organization, Geneva, July.

Lee, Byung-Hee, and Seong-mi Jeong. 2008. "Non-standard Workers of Korea: Changes in Size and Composition." Working paper, Korea Labor Institute, *e-Labor News* 80 (March).

Lee, Chulhee. 2002. "Structural Changes in Household Income Inequality in Korea: A New Decomposition including Labor Supply Changes." *Seoul Journal of Economics* (Fall).

Lee, Joung-woo, and Seong-hyeon Hwang. 1998. "The Problems of Income Distribution and Related Policy Issues in Korea." *KDI Journal of Economic Policy* 20, no. 1–2, 153–230.

Lee, Kye Woo, and Chanyong Park. 2002. "Globalization, Growth, Inequality, and Social Safety Nets in APEC Economies." *Asian Development Review* 19, no. 2, 47–66.

Lee, Woosung. 2000. "Unequal Asset Ownership and Increasing Income Inequality." *Weekly Economy* 594, LG Economic Research Institute, Seoul (in Korean).

Leipziger, Danny, David Dollar, and A. F. Shorrocks. 1992. *The Distribution of Income and Wealth in Korea*. Washington, DC: World Bank.

Lim, Byung-In, and Jin Kwon Hyun. 2009. "What Makes the Income Tax System So Progressive? A Case of Korea." *Applied Economics Letters* 16, no. 11, 683–687.

Lim, Byung-In, and Seung-hoon Jeon. 2005. "The Analysis on Income Inequality within Corhort." Paper presented at Sixth Korea Labor Income Panel Study Conference, Seoul, February.

Lu, Jui-fen, Gabriel Leung, Soonman Kwon, Keith Y. K. Tin, Eddy Van Doorslaer, and Owen O'Donnell. 2007. "Horizontal Equity in Health Care Utilization: Evidence from Three High-Income Asian Economies." *Social Science and Medicine* 64, 199–212.

Ministry of Employment and Labor. 2009. *Report on Occupational Wage Survey*. Micro-data set, 2008 and prior years.

Ministry of Health, Welfare and Family Affairs (MIHWFA). 2008. Basic Old-Age Pension. See http://english.mw.go.kr.

Ministry of Strategy and Finance. 2010. *National Budget Plan*. Available at: http://search.korea.net:8080/intro_korea2008/society/pdf/01_11.pdf.

Moon, Hyungpyo. 2003. "The Korean Pension System: Current State and Tasks Ahead." Mimeo, Korea Development Institute (Seoul).

———. 2008. "The Role of Social Pensions in Korea." Paper presented at World Bank–MOF–Hitotsubashi Workshop, Closing the Coverage Gap: The Role of Social Pensions, Tokyo, February.

National Health Insurance Corporation (NHIC). 2007. *2007 National Health Insurance Program of Korea*. Seoul: NHIC, January.

National Pension Fund Institute. 2008. "Long-Term Projections," November.

National Pension Service. 2008. *Amendment to the National Pension Act, 2007*, http://www.nps.or.kr/.

Organization for Economic Cooperation and Development (OECD). 2003. *OECD Reviews of Health Care Systems: Korea*. Paris: OECD.

———. 2007a. *Social Expenditure Data Base 2007*. Paris: OECD.

———. 2007b. *Society at a Glance, 2006 Edition*. Paris: OECD.

———. 2008a. *Growing Unequal? Income Distribution and Poverty in OECD Countries*. Paris: OECD.

———. 2008b. *OECD Employment Outlook*. Paris: OECD.

————. 2010a. *Health Data 2008*. Paris: OECD.

————. 2010b. *Revenue Statistics*. Paris: OECD.

Park, Chanyong. 2002. "Poverty and Socio-Economic Change in Korea." Working Paper 02-2-3, Korea Institute for Health and Social Affairs, Seoul.

Park, In Hwa, and Dug Man Lee. 2008. "Policy Agenda for the Improvement of the Efficiency of the Welfare Budget." *Korean Social Security Studies* 24, no. 4, 33–63 (in Korean).

Park, Sungjun. 2000. "Earning Inequality in Korea after the Financial Crisis." *Korean Journal of Labor Economics* 23, no. 2, 61–80.

Pechman, Joseph A., and Benjamin A. Okner. 1974. *Who Bears the Tax Burden?* Washington, DC: Brookings Institution.

Perotti, Roberto. 1996. "Growth, Income Distribution, and Democracy: What the Data Say." *Journal of Economic Growth* 1, no. 2, 149–187.

Persson, Torsten, and Guido Tabellini. 1994. "Is Inequality Harmful for Growth?" *American Economic Review* 84, no. 3 (June), 600–621.

Pfähler, Wilhelm. 1990. "Redistributive Effect of Income Taxation: Decomposing Tax Base and Tax Rate Effects." *Bulletin of Economic Research* 42, no. 2, 121–129.

Republic of China. 2007. *Report on the Survey of Family Income and Expenditure in Taiwan Area of Republic of China*. Micro-survey files for 2006 and prior years.

Reynolds, Morgan, and Eugene Smolensky. 1977. *Public Expenditures, Taxes, and the Distribution of Income*. New York: Academic Press.

Ruger, Jennifer Prah, and Hak-Ju Kim. 2007. "Out-of-Pocket Healthcare Spending by the Poor and Chronically Ill in the Republic of Korea." *American Journal of Public Health* 97, no. 5, 804–811.

Shorrocks, A. F. 1978. "The Measurement of Mobility." *Econometrica* 46, no. 5, 1013–1024.

Song, Young Joo. 2009. "The South Korean Health Care System." *Japan Medical Association Journal* 52, no. 3, 206–209.

Suh, Sang-Mok, and Ha-cheong Yeon. 1986. "Social Welfare during the Structural Adjustment Period in Korea." Working Paper 8604, Korea Development Institute, Seoul.

Sung, Myung Jae. 2001. "Changes in Income Distribution of Urban Households and Their Determinants in Korea." Research Report 01-01, Korea Institute of Public Finance (in Korean).

————. 2009. "The Effects of Taxes and Benefits on Income Distribution and Poverty Rates in Korea." Paper presented at the 65th Annual Conference of the International Institute of Public Finance, Cape Town, August.

————. 2010. "Population Aging, Mobility of Quarterly Incomes, and Annual Income Inequality: Theoretical Discussion and Empirical Findings." Paper presented at the 66th Annual Congress of the International Institute of Public Finance, Uppsala, August.

———. 2011. "Changes in Income Distribution and Redistributive Effects of Tax/Fiscal Policies in Korea." Unpublished manuscript, Korea Institute of Public Finance.

Sung, Myung Jae, and Ki-baeg Park. 2009. "Effects of Demographic Changes on Income Inequality in Korea." *Kyong Je Hak Yon Gu* 57, no. 4, 5–37.

———. 2011. "Effects of Taxes and Benefits on Income Distribution in Korea." *Review of Income and Wealth* 57, no. 2, 345–363.

United States Census Bureau. 2009. Current Population Survey, Annual Social and Economic Supplements. Micro-survey data for 2008 and prior years.

Wagstaff, Adam, and Eddy van Doorslaer. 2001. "What Makes the Personal Income Tax Progressive? A Comparative Analysis for Fifteen OECD Countries." *International Tax and Public Finance* 8, 299–315.

Weisbrod, Burton A. 1970. "Collective Action and the Distribution of Income: A Conceptual Approach." In R. H. Haveman and J. Margolis, eds., *Public Expenditures and Policy Analysis*, 117–141. Chicago: Markham Publishing Company.

World Bank. 2002. "Data Base for Development Analysis: An Overview." In *World Economy.* Washington, DC: World Bank.

———. 2004. "The Republic of Korea: Four Decades of Equitable Growth." World Bank Working Paper 30781, May. Available online at World Bank Documents and Reports.

———. 2010. World Development Indicators. Available at http://elibrary.worldbank.org/.

Yoo, Gyungjoon. 1998. "The Analysis of Decomposition of Wage Income Inequality and Its Causes." *KDI Journal of Economic Policy* 20, no. 3/4, 267–312.

Yoo, Ilho. 1997. "An Estimate of the Tax Evasion in Korea: Income and Value Added Taxes." Working Paper 97-03, Korea Institute of Public Finance, August.

Yoon, Gijoong. 1997. *The Analysis of Income Inequality in Korea.* Seoul: Pakyoung-Sa (in Korean).

Index

Harvard East Asian Monographs
(*out-of-print)

Harvard East Asian Monographs

Harvard East Asian Monographs

Harvard East Asian Monographs

170. Denise Potrzeba Lett, *In Pursuit of Status: The Making of South Korea's "New" Urban Middle Class*

171. Mimi Hall Yiengpruksawan, *Hiraizumi: Buddhist Art and Regional Politics in Twelfth-Century Japan*

172. Charles Shirō Inouye, *The Similitude of Blossoms: A Critical Biography of Izumi Kyōka (1873–1939), Japanese Novelist and Playwright*

173. Aviad E. Raz, *Riding the Black Ship: Japan and Tokyo Disneyland*

174. Deborah J. Milly, *Poverty, Equality, and Growth: The Politics of Economic Need in Postwar Japan*

175. See Heng Teow, *Japan's Cultural Policy Toward China, 1918–1931: A Comparative Perspective*

176. Michael A. Fuller, *An Introduction to Literary Chinese*

177. Frederick R. Dickinson, *War and National Reinvention: Japan in the Great War, 1914–1919*

178. John Solt, *Shredding the Tapestry of Meaning: The Poetry and Poetics of Kitasono Katue (1902–1978)*

179. Edward Pratt, *Japan's Protoindustrial Elite: The Economic Foundations of the Gōnō*

180. Atsuko Sakaki, *Recontextualizing Texts: Narrative Performance in Modern Japanese Fiction*

181. Soon-Won Park, *Colonial Industrialization and Labor in Korea: The Onoda Cement Factory*

182. JaHyun Kim Haboush and Martina Deuchler, *Culture and the State in Late Chosŏn Korea*

183. John W. Chaffee, *Branches of Heaven: A History of the Imperial Clan of Sung China*

184. Gi-Wook Shin and Michael Robinson, eds., *Colonial Modernity in Korea*

185. Nam-lin Hur, *Prayer and Play in Late Tokugawa Japan: Asakusa Sensōji and Edo Society*

186. Kristin Stapleton, *Civilizing Chengdu: Chinese Urban Reform, 1895–1937*

187. Hyung Il Pai, *Constructing "Korean" Origins: A Critical Review of Archaeology, Historiography, and Racial Myth in Korean State-Formation Theories*

188. Brian D. Ruppert, *Jewel in the Ashes: Buddha Relics and Power in Early Medieval Japan*

189. Susan Daruvala, *Zhou Zuoren and an Alternative Chinese Response to Modernity*

*190. James Z. Lee, *The Political Economy of a Frontier: Southwest China, 1250–1850*

191. Kerry Smith, *A Time of Crisis: Japan, the Great Depression, and Rural Revitalization*

192. Michael Lewis, *Becoming Apart: National Power and Local Politics in Toyama, 1868–1945*

193. William C. Kirby, Man-houng Lin, James Chin Shih, and David A. Pietz, eds., *State and Economy in Republican China: A Handbook for Scholars*

194. Timothy S. George, *Minamata: Pollution and the Struggle for Democracy in Postwar Japan*

195. Billy K. L. So, *Prosperity, Region, and Institutions in Maritime China: The South Fukien Pattern, 946–1368*

196. Yoshihisa Tak Matsusaka, *The Making of Japanese Manchuria, 1904–1932*

Harvard East Asian Monographs

197. Maram Epstein, *Competing Discourses: Orthodoxy, Authenticity, and Engendered Meanings in Late Imperial Chinese Fiction*
198. Curtis J. Milhaupt, J. Mark Ramseyer, and Michael K. Young, eds. and comps., *Japanese Law in Context: Readings in Society, the Economy, and Politics*
199. Haruo Iguchi, *Unfinished Business: Ayukawa Yoshisuke and U.S.-Japan Relations, 1937–1952*
200. Scott Pearce, Audrey Spiro, and Patricia Ebrey, *Culture and Power in the Reconstitution of the Chinese Realm, 200–600*
201. Terry Kawashima, *Writing Margins: The Textual Construction of Gender in Heian and Kamakura Japan*
202. Martin W. Huang, *Desire and Fictional Narrative in Late Imperial China*
203. Robert S. Ross and Jiang Changbin, eds., *Re-examining the Cold War: U.S.-China Diplomacy, 1954–1973*
204. Guanhua Wang, *In Search of Justice: The 1905–1906 Chinese Anti-American Boycott*
205. David Schaberg, *A Patterned Past: Form and Thought in Early Chinese Historiography*
206. Christine Yano, *Tears of Longing: Nostalgia and the Nation in Japanese Popular Song*
207. Milena Doleželová-Velingerová and Oldřich Král, with Graham Sanders, eds., *The Appropriation of Cultural Capital: China's May Fourth Project*
208. Robert N. Huey, *The Making of 'Shinkokinshū'*
209. Lee Butler, *Emperor and Aristocracy in Japan, 1467–1680: Resilience and Renewal*
210. Suzanne Ogden, *Inklings of Democracy in China*
211. Kenneth J. Ruoff, *The People's Emperor: Democracy and the Japanese Monarchy, 1945–1995*
212. Haun Saussy, *Great Walls of Discourse and Other Adventures in Cultural China*
213. Aviad E. Raz, *Emotions at Work: Normative Control, Organizations, and Culture in Japan and America*
214. Rebecca E. Karl and Peter Zarrow, eds., *Rethinking the 1898 Reform Period: Political and Cultural Change in Late Qing China*
215. Kevin O'Rourke, *The Book of Korean Shijo*
216. Ezra F. Vogel, ed., *The Golden Age of the U.S.-China-Japan Triangle, 1972–1989*
217. Thomas A. Wilson, ed., *On Sacred Grounds: Culture, Society, Politics, and the Formation of the Cult of Confucius*
218. Donald S. Sutton, *Steps of Perfection: Exorcistic Performers and Chinese Religion in Twentieth-Century Taiwan*
219. Daqing Yang, *Technology of Empire: Telecommunications and Japanese Expansionism in Asia, 1883–1945*
220. Qianshen Bai, *Fu Shan's World: The Transformation of Chinese Calligraphy in the Seventeenth Century*
221. Paul Jakov Smith and Richard von Glahn, eds., *The Song-Yuan-Ming Transition in Chinese History*
222. Rania Huntington, *Alien Kind: Foxes and Late Imperial Chinese Narrative*
223. Jordan Sand, *House and Home in Modern Japan: Architecture, Domestic Space, and Bourgeois Culture, 1880–1930*

Harvard East Asian Monographs